Comput

MW00427594

Implementation and Explanation

(with OpenGL/GLSL/C++)

Jules Bloomenthal

All illustrations and images in this text are either the work of the author, used with permission, or within the public domain.

The cover image of faces is figure 15-2.

To my wife Julie, and our daughter Kira

Contents

Part 2: Flexed Text
Bonus

Preface

This book presents the essential theory, mathematics, and software needed for a modern and complete graphics application. It is designed for an upper-level, college course in computer graphics programming and develops techniques through a series of exercises.

The "shader architecture" to which this book subscribes allows programmers to create complex scenes on everyday computers. It exposes virtually all graphical data, thus providing numerous pedagogical opportunities. All the theoretical concepts and mathematics developed in this text are demonstrated with working implementations.

Examples and exercises use C++, OpenGL, and GLSL. The exercises are incremental and designed to develop skill and understanding. They may be challenging, but not, it is hoped, unduly difficult.

Rather than survey the wide range of techniques, this book focuses on the most basic and useful, presenting the material in as direct a path as possible. Render engines, game engines, and other higher-level programming methods are not discussed; instead, this book seeks to demonstrate that ab initio software can be as effective.

A brief history of computer graphics is offered to provide context for modern techniques. Seminal contributions are acknowledged, but for each person mentioned in this text, many others have also contributed.

Jules Bloomenthal
Seattle, Washington

Chapter 1: Introduction

Computer graphics is the processing (*rendering*) of geometry (usually two- or three-dimensional *vertices*) to a display (usually an array of *pixels*). *Interactive, real-time* computer graphics implies a minimum of ten or so new *frames* (displays) each second, with the difference between frames resulting from animation or user Interaction.

Computer graphics is rich in theory, with algorithms that achieve speed and quality over a wide range of visual features and practical applications.

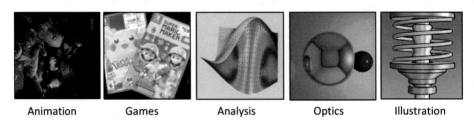

Animation	Games	Analysis	Optics	Illustration

Figure 1-1: A Large Domain of Applications
Animation is from *The Storyteller* (courtesy Lon Koenig Games)
Illustration is from *A Non-Photorealistic Lighting Model for Automatic
Technical Illustration* (courtesy Gooch, Gooch, Shirley and Cohen)

The software architecture is, however, complicated. It requires the graphics programmer to grapple with many arcane details. But its mastery yields a universe of possibilities.

This book describes modern, shader architecture, as embodied by *OpenGL* (a freely available application programming interface) and *GLSL* (a graphics shading language). In this chapter we describe the technical requirements, software contexts, and rationale for modern graphics programming practice.

First, let us briefly acknowledge the true meaning of computer graphics.

Magic

Computer graphics conjures an image; like *magic*, it is illusion. It can recreate a memory, a dream, or a design. Graphics programmers transform mental images into visual reality; they apply principles of light and geometry in their software to represent, manipulate, display, and even manufacture objects.

1

If there is one central role in the magic of computer graphics, it is the surface normal, the direction a surface is facing. It is a direction we understand, one we can manipulate, and with which we can produce a shaded image.

Like magic, there are many techniques to master.

1.1 Modern Graphics Programming

With the new millennium, graphics programming became more complex. There was a shift to "shader architecture", which requires programming of the *graphics processing unit* (GPU). To understand the rationale and impact of this architecture, a brief review of graphics development is helpful.

First Line Drawings, then Shaded Images

For his 1963 doctoral dissertation, Ivan Sutherland developed *Sketchpad*, the first and most influential computer graphics program. The display was an oscilloscope connected to computer-controlled digital-to-analog converters. A few years later, at Harvard, Sutherland and colleagues developed the first virtual reality display. Both devices were *line drawing*.

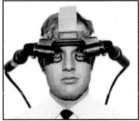

Figure 1-2: left: Ivan Sutherland and Sketchpad at Lincoln Lab, 1963
right: first virtual reality head-mounted display, Harvard, 1967

Line drawings could be ambiguous and confusing, however. Greater realism required *shaded images*. These were first produced with a film recorder: a non-real-time display exposed film, scan line (a horizontal row) by scan line. This required ordering objects for each scan line, and, thus, initially there was considerable emphasis on sorting methods.

Shaded display at interactive rates and/or rendering in random order required a new memory device: a rectangular *raster* of picture elements (*pixels*). The first such devices

2

(or *frame buffers*) were built in 1969 (General Electric), 1972 (Xerox PARC), and 1974 (Evans & Sutherland).

With a frame buffer, pixels internal to, e.g., a triangle, are assigned values, and those values are retrieved from memory and converted to a video signal during display. The addition of an ancillary raster, the *z-buffer*, eliminated many sorting requirements.

Figure 1-3: *SuperPaint* by Dick Shoup, 1972
(courtesy the Computer History Museum)

Hardware and OpenGL

Through the 1970s, special-purpose hardware was used to produce shaded images of three-dimensional objects at interactive rates. In 1981, while teaching at Stanford University, Jim Clark developed the *geometry engine*, the first VLSI circuit to support common graphical operations. He founded Silicon Graphics (SGI), and produced the first interactive graphics workstation affordable by computer science departments and modestly sized businesses.

Figure 1-4: Jim Clark and a geometry engine
(used with permission)

3

In the early 1980s, SGI developed a graphics library, *GL*, for its workstations. In 1992 it released an 'open' version, *OpenGL*, providing a standard for graphics development.

OpenGL (version 1) is an API that provides control for basic shading, lighting, camera, and texturing functions. Advanced methods (such as Phong shading, demonstrated in 1974) could not be supported in real-time by SGI hardware (not in 1982 when GL was written, nor in 1992, when OpenGL was released). Version 1 was, however, satisfactory for many graphical applications through the 1990s.

Renderman

For applications in which image quality was paramount, such as production animation, non-interactive (i.e., software, not hardware) methods were developed. In his 1984 paper, *Shade Trees*, Rob Cook proposed a *shader architecture* consisting of *shader programs* ("shaders") to associate with geometric objects. The new architecture permitted greater control over graphical processes.

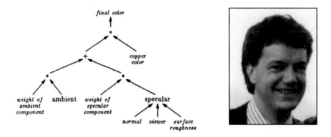

Figure 1-5: Shade tree for copper; Rob Cook
(used with permission)

The architecture was developed into Pixar's Renderman, a software renderer released in 1990. It supported a graphics language for the shader programs. One of its architects, Pat Hanrahan, explained, "Modeling the optical properties of real material requires the full generality of a programming language … [as opposed to] a single large parameterized shading model."

Depending on scene and shading complexity, Renderman required substantial computation time. In response, Pixar created a multi-computer "render farm" to produce the first fully computer-generated feature animation, *Toy Story*.

Figure 1-6: Ed Catmull and Pixar's render farm, 1995
(used with permission)

GPU Hardware

Also in the early 1990s, Nvidia Corp. developed graphics circuitry with an ever-increasing number of processors. When a large number of vertices must be processed and a large number of pixels must be computed, the vertex and pixel calculations are parceled amongst the processors, greatly increasing overall throughput.

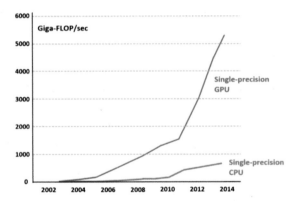

Figure 1-7: Computational power of the CPU and the GPU
(source: Nvidia CUDA Programming Guide)

The modern GPU is the most powerful computational device in today's commercial market, and its power continues to increase. In 2012 a high-end laptop GPU had 350 processors. Five years later, the comparable product had 2500.

Changes to the API

With the programmable GPUs released after 2000, real-time rendering possibilities dramatically expanded. These new possibilities required three significant changes to graphics programming.

1) With increased computational power, the range of real-time techniques expanded beyond any one shading model. Accordingly, since version 2, OpenGL does not provide a default shading or viewing model. *Transformations, lighting, and shading were deleted from the API and became the responsibility of the graphics programmer.*

2) To execute software on the GPU, "shader programs" must be written a shading language (like GLSL), downloaded to the GPU, compiled, linked and executed. *This introduced an additional layer to the software.*

3) Internal GPU bus speeds are much greater than CPU/GPU transfer rates; to prevent bottlenecks, vertex data was required to reside in GPU memory. *Arrangement of and access to GPU memory became the responsibility of the programmer.*

These changes underlie the reputation of modern graphics programming as challenging.

Is Shader Architecture Better?

OpenGL version 2 allows the graphics programmer to control the GPU and to access virtually all variables affecting graphical processes. With this access and with the expressive power of the shading language, the programmer can create interactive, complex, and high-quality imagery on a laptop (and, somewhat, on a cellphone).

This improved access also improves pedagogy. In this book we are able to demonstrate with working software virtually every theoretical development presented.

The non-programmer too has remarkable access. Consider the web browser. In 2006 Google Earth was able to display textured 3D buildings. In 2011 WebGL allowed HTML commands to access the GPU. Most web browsers now support shader architecture.

Figure 1-8: Advanced graphics execution on a web browser
(source: GoogleMaps)

Since 2013 the Firefox debugger has been able to display GLSL code as it executes on
the GPU. If the user invokes the debugger (F-12) and selects "Shader Editor", the code is
displayed, and can be edited.

For example, the code below, which is executed for each pixel, tests whether a point on
the table is in shadow. If it is, the pixel intensity is dimmed by 50%, in the code at left. At
right, the intensity scalar was manually edited to 1.5, yielding a 'bright shadow'.

```
if (doShadow == 1) {
    float a = RaySphere(v_point, L, vec4(ball
    if (a >= 0.)
        intensity = .5*intensity;
}
```

```
if (doShadow == 1) {
    float a = RaySphere(v_point, L, vec4(ball
    if (a >= 0.)
        intensity = 1.5*intensity;
}
```

Figure 1-9: GLSL on a browser

Unfortunately, applications and WebGL programs require a good deal more than the
Firefox debugger. In the exercises in this text, the programmer must cobble together all
the pieces necessary for an executable application.

Other APIs

Virtually all GPU manufacturers support OpenGL, and all major languages provide OpenGL bindings. Other APIs that support a shader architecture include DirectX (Microsoft) and Metal (Apple).

This text provides only OpenGL examples. Macintosh programmers may be able to use Bootcamp to access OpenGL drivers. Or, all but one or two exercises can be implemented with WebGL, which should run on any modern web browser.

Future developments may alter the computational structure of computer graphics, but, for now, shader architecture appears to be a stable platform.

1.2 Resources

Text Materials

This text develops graphics techniques through a series of exercises. They can be solved with the text and its code fragments, as well as libraries, application examples, and sample data files on *www.bloomenthal.com* (login as *Reader*, with password *imagination*). The online examples provide considerable guidance in the solution of exercises.

It isn't practical to provide specifications for OpenGL subroutines; we describe only a few in detail. The OpenGL and GLSL reference *www.khronos.org/registry/OpenGL-Refpages* provides detailed descriptions, as well as a colorfully organized reference card.

The web offers numerous tutorials and abundant commentary about OpenGL, but seldom error-free. Several websites and twitter accounts are devoted to sharing innovative shaders and applications.

The standard, comprehensive reference is *Computer Graphics: Principles and Practice* by Foley, van Dam, et al. There are numerous introductory, advanced, and reference texts devoted to OpenGL.

Beginning in 1973, *SIGGRAPH*, a special interest group in graphics, of the Association of Computing Machinery (ACM), has sponsored a yearly conference at which the year's most innovative work is presented. Academicians, researchers, equipment manufacturers, leaders in animation and other graphics related areas gather, providing opportunities for students to connect with the industry.

Figure 1-10: *Inside a Quark*, cover art, 1984 SIGGRAPH Proceedings
(courtesy Ned Greene)

Graphics advances are no longer reserved for production houses, studios, 3D tool developers, game companies, and computer science departments. They can now be implemented by individuals using consumer-level computers and freely available APIs.

Chapter 2: Nut, Meet Bolt

The specific requirements of a graphics application are best understood in terms of the underlying implementation of most graphics architectures: the *graphics pipeline*.

2.1 The Graphics Pipeline

The calculation of pixel values involves a pipeline of operations. Simplified, there are four stages:

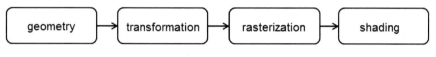

Figure 2-1: Simplified graphics pipeline

1) **Geometry** is typically defined by *vertices*, which are two- or three-dimensional locations (with optional attributes such as color). Vertices are 'fed' into the pipeline to form a primitive, i.e, three or four vertices that represent a triangle or quadrilateral (henceforth, "quad").

2) **Transformation** applies a view ("camera") to determine the display location of the vertices.

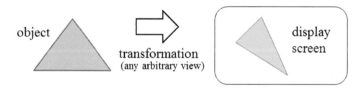

Figure 2-2: Transformed geometry

3) **Rasterization** determines those pixels covered by the transformed primitive (triangle or quad). This is shown below, where a pixel is a point at the intersection of a row and column (a pixel is *not* a rectangle bounded by the lines).

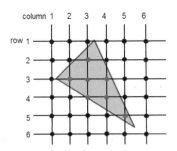

Figure 2-3: Pixels (in green) covered by a triangle

4) **Shading** occurs for each covered pixel; that is, *rgba* (red, green, and blue for color, and alpha for opacity) values are assigned to individual pixels.

Rasterization is a tedious process that, fortunately, OpenGL implements for us. The other stages, however, are the responsibility of the developer.

2.2 Example: Clearing the Screen (version 1)

Our first example uses OpenGL version 1, which does not subscribe to shader architecture. In the next section, we compare it with a shader-based implementation.

Figure 2-4: First example

The following code, 1-Example-ClearScreen-v1.cpp, implements three stages of the graphics pipeline: stage 1 sets the vertex grouping to four and sends four vertices into the pipeline; stage 2 is implied (OpenGL version 1 maintains a camera transformation that defaults to identity); and stage 4 calls *glColor*. Stage 3, rasterization, is performed by OpenGL and requires no implementation by the programmer. A discussion follows.

```
// 1-Example-ClearScreen-v1.cpp - OpenGL v1

#include "glad.h"         // GL definitions - must precede glfw3.h
#include <GLFW/glfw3.h>   // application toolkit - access to window mgr
```

11

```
#include <stdio.h>          // for getchar

int main() {
    // initialize toolkit, create window
    glfwInit();
    GLFWwindow *w = glfwCreateWindow(300, 300, "Clear", NULL, NULL);
    // establish GL context for this window
    glfwMakeContextCurrent(w);
    // establish GL subroutine pointers
    gladLoadGLLoader((GLADloadproc) glfwGetProcAddress);
    // define a vertex 'attribute' (ie, green)
    glColor3d(0, 1, 0);
    // define a square object
    glBegin(GL_QUADS);
    glVertex2d(-1, -1);
    glVertex2d(-1, 1);
    glVertex2d(1, 1);
    glVertex2d(1, -1);
    glEnd();
    // complete all GL operations, swap double-buffered frame
    glFlush();
    glfwSwapBuffers(w);
    // wait for user keystroke to exit
    getchar();
}
```

Discussion

ClearScreen depends on three libraries: *stdio* supports the call to getchar, *glfw3* supports window creation and OpenGL initialization, and *glad* accommodates the specific OpenGL version supported by the GPU.

Instructions regarding needed libraries are included with the first exercise, at the end of this chapter.

Let's briefly consider GLFW and GLAD.

GLFW: an OpenGL Toolkit

A graphics *toolkit* is a library that negotiates with the operating system to create an application window and then an OpenGL context for the window. Our examples use GLFW, a "Graphics Library Framework". In addition to supporting the graphics display, GLFW provides *callback* mechanisms for keyboard and mouse input. Alternate toolkits include GLUT (a.k.a. freeglut), SDL, and QT. GLUT and GLFW are basic, i.e., 'bare-bones'.

GLAD: an OpenGL Loader

The definitions for the callable subroutines in the OpenGL library depend on the OpenGL version(s) supported by the GPU. These definitions must be loaded before compilation; subroutine pointers are then established at run-time.

A popular means to do this is with GLEW (the GL Extension Wrangler); it has, however, flaws and may fail with some compilers. An alternative is a custom loader (see www.khronos.org/opengl/wiki/OpenGL_Loading_Library).

Perhaps the simplest means is to use a website (such as http://glad.dav1d.de/) to generate appropriate definition files. The examples in this book use GLAD (see exercise 1 for detailed instructions).

2.3 Example: Clearing the Screen (version 2)

OpenGL, version 2 (released 2004) and beyond, feature *shader architecture*. Major elements are related in the diagram below.

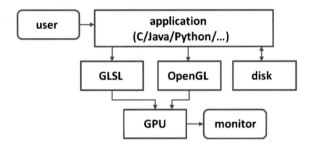

Figure 2-5: Organization of a shader application

This architecture requires the programmer to write shader programs in the Graphics Library Shading Language (GLSL). The application must load GLSL code into the GPU, manage the graphics state through calls to OpenGL, respond to user input, and access any needed files from disk.

The example below is annotated regarding the three requirements (sec. 1.5) for shader architecture:

1) transformation and shading,
2) download and execution of shading language code, and
3) transfer of vertex data.

13

The library GLXtras.h is added to simplify some shader operations. GLSL defines a basic type, **vec2**, which is used as an input to the vertex shader below.

```cpp
// 1-Example-ClearScreen-v2.cpp - use OpenGL shader architecture

#include <glad.h>                         // GL headers
#include <glfw3.h>                        // GL toolkit
#include <stdio.h>                        // getchar, printf, etc.
#include "GLXtras.h"                      // convenience routines

GLuint vBuffer = 0;                       // GPU buf ID, valid if > 0
GLuint program = 0;                       // shader ID, valid if > 0

// vertex shader: operations before the rasterizer
const char *vertexShader = "\
    #version 130                                                  \n\
    in vec2 point;                        // 2D pt from GPU memory \n\
    void main() {                                                 \n\
        // REQUIREMENT 1A) transform vertex:                      \n\
        gl_Position = vec4(point, 0, 1);    // 'built-in' variable \n\
    }";

// pixel shader: operations after the rasterizer
const char *pixelShader = "\
    #version 130                                                  \n\
    out vec4 pColor;                                              \n\
    void main() {                                                 \n\
        // REQUIREMENT 1B) shade pixel:                           \n\
        pColor = vec4(0, 1, 0, 1);          // r, g, b, alpha     \n\
    }";

void InitVertexBuffer() {
    // REQUIRMENT 3A) create GPU buffer, copy 4 vertices
    float pts[][2] = {{-1,-1},{-1,1},{1,1},{1,-1}}; // square 'object'
    glGenBuffers(1, &vBuffer);                // ID for GPU buffer
    glBindBuffer(GL_ARRAY_BUFFER, vBuffer); // make it active
    glBufferData(GL_ARRAY_BUFFER, sizeof(pts), pts, GL_STATIC_DRAW);
}

void Display() {
    glUseProgram(program);                  // set local shader
    glBindBuffer(GL_ARRAY_BUFFER, vBuffer); // activate vertex buffer
    // REQUIREMENT 3B) set vertex feeder
    VertexAttribPointer(program, "point", 2, 0, (void *) 0);
    glDrawArrays(GL_QUADS, 0, 4);           // draw entire window
    glFlush();                              // flush GL ops
}
```

```c
void Keyboard(GLFWwindow *w, int key, int scancode, int action, int mods) {
    // test for exit
    if (key == GLFW_KEY_ESCAPE && action == GLFW_PRESS)
        glfwSetWindowShouldClose(w, GLFW_TRUE);
}

void GlfwError(int id, const char *reason) {
    printf("GLFW error %i: %s\n", id, reason);
}

void APIENTRY GlslError(GLenum source, GLenum type, GLuint id,
    GLenum severity, GLsizei len, const GLchar *msg, const void *data) {
        printf("GLSL Error: %s\n", msg);
}

int AppError(const char *msg) {
    glfwTerminate();
    printf("Error: %s\n", msg);
    return 1;
}

int main() {                                // application entry
    glfwSetErrorCallback(GlfwError);        // init GL toolkit
    if (!glfwInit())
        return 1;
    // create named window of given size
    GLFWwindow *w = glfwCreateWindow(300, 300, "Clear", NULL, NULL);
    if (!w)
        return AppError("can't open window");
    glfwMakeContextCurrent(w);
    // set OpenGL extensions
    gladLoadGLLoader((GLADloadproc) glfwGetProcAddress);
    // *** following line compiles only for OpenGLv4.3+
    glDebugMessageCallback(GlslError, NULL);
    // REQUIREMENT 2) build shader program
    if (!(program = LinkProgramViaCode(&vertexShader, &pixelShader)))
        return AppError("can't link shader program");
    InitVertexBuffer();                     // set GPU vertex memory
    glfwSetKeyCallback(w, Keyboard);        // establish callback
    while (!glfwWindowShouldClose(w)) {     // event loop
        Display();
        if (PrintGLErrors())                // runtime GL error test
            getchar();                      // if error, pause
        glfwSwapBuffers(w);                 // swap double-buffered frame
        glfwPollEvents();
    }
    glfwDestroyWindow(w);
    glfwTerminate();
}
```

Discussion

The shader example, 1-Example-ClearScreen-v2.cpp, is quite a bit longer than the first version. It would be even longer but for its use of *VertexAttribPointer*, *PrintGLErrors*, and *LinkProgramViaCode*, which are convenience subroutines in GLXtras.h.

In the application's *main*, several GLFW calls establish the application window followed by a call to *gladLoadGLLoader*, which establishes addresses for those OpenGL extensions supported by the particular GPU executing the software.

The vertex and pixel shader strings are compiled and linked in *main*, and vertex data is transferred by a call to *InitVertexBuffer*. A callback subroutine is registered for keyboard events; it terminates the application in response to an <ESC> keypress. *main* enters an "event loop", which polls for any user input and redraws the display.

Display arranges for the GPU data to be fed to the "point" input of the vertex shader via a call to *VertexAttribPointer*. Its arguments (after identifying the program and the input name) include the number of components of the data (in this case, 2 for two-dimensional), distance in bytes between adjacent points, and any offset into the data,

Display then calls *glDrawArrays* in order to send the four buffered vertices to the vertex shader. These form a single quadrilateral, i.e., the entire screen, which is then rasterized. The result is every pixel being shaded by the pixel shader.

GLSL

The syntax and semantics of GLSL are similar to C, but without pointers.

GLSL supports several basic types in addition to **int** and **float**; in this text we'll use **vec2**, **vec3**, and **vec4** (corresponding to vectors in 2, 3, and 4 dimensions) and **mat4** (a 4-by-4 matrix, described in chapter 6). The vector and matrix elements are single-precision floats (i.e., 32 bits). They correspond with the C++ vector and matrix types defined in VecMat.h.

The application and all the shaders begin execution with a subroutine named "main", which can be confusing but meaning of the term is usually clear from context.

Versions

Between the release of OpenGL v2.1 (and GLSL v1.1) in 2004 and the release of OpenGL v4.5 (and GLSL v4.5) in 2012, increased functionality was carefully and incrementally introduced. The examples in this text should all function with OpenGL v2.1 and GLSL v1.3 (perhaps v1.2), with the exception that examples in chapter 19 (the geometry shader) require OpenGLv3 and examples in chapter 20 (tessellation) require OpenGLv4.

The GLSL version used by the GPU is determined by the #version statement of a shader. It is reasonable to reduce the version number as much as possible, allowing the code to run on more hardware. But version 110 code that runs on one machine may not run on another. This can result in initial error statements such as "incorrect GLSL version" or "extension not available in current GLSL version".

Thus, the minimum GLSL version specified in this text is 130.

Error Handling

There are three levels of error handling in the previous example.

Initialization errors are detected in *main* if there is a problem opening the window or if the shader program fails to build. Runtime OpenGL errors are detected in *Display* by a call to *PrintGLErrors*, which is defined in GLXtras.h.

It is during execution of the application that the shader program is built. If there are any type mismatches or undefined usages, or any runtime GLSL errors, error messages will appear when the program is run, in the console window. They can be cryptic compared to C++ compiler errors.

With OpenGL 4.3, "developer-friendly debug outputs" were provided for the GPU. This is done in *main* by registering an error callback using *glDebugMessageCallback*. This subroutine is undefined (and should not be called) with earlier versions of OpenGL.

A GLSL coding error will likely produce subsequent runtime failures, such as the inability to locate shader input variables. These runtime errors quickly consume the console window, obscuring the initial error report. This can be remedied by adding a call to *getchar* in every error routine.

For brevity, the remaining examples omit error handling.

OpenGL Inconsistencies

The OpenGL API is designed for efficient programming despite its awkward (at times) naming conventions. It was written for C, not C++, and so does not support subroutine overloading (thus, for example, there are 68 subroutines with a name beginning "glAttrib"). The binding mechanism can also be awkward.

There are arcane differences in variables for closely related OpenGL subroutines; these inconsistencies can lead to programming errors that are difficult to locate. www.khronos.org/opengl/wiki can be helpful in this regard.

2.4 Exercise

Part 1: Setup

This exercise is to modify ClearScreen so that it draws a chessboard. The book website contains OpenGL setup instructions, a very short VersionGL test program, and 2-Example-ClearScreen-v2.cpp.

Part 2: VersionGL

After setup, compile and run VersionGL.cpp, a simple program to determine your computer's GPU and its capabilities regarding OpenGL.

Part 3: Chessboard

Rename a copy of 2-Example-ClearScreen.cpp to Chessboard.cpp. Now, modify it so that, rather than clear the screen, it draws a chessboard of eight columns and eight rows, with alternating black and white squares. *This only requires changes to the pixel shader* (the final pixel shader is about 10 lines).

Hints

a) Use "built-in" pixel shader variable *gl_FragCoord* (the pixel coordinates). The window should be 400 by 400 pixels, so *gl_FragCoord.x* and *gl_FragCoord.y* should range from 0 to 400 (and a checkerboard square should be 50 by 50 pixels).

b) Create a subroutine *Odd* that determines whether an input integer is odd or even; this subroutine may be defined immediately before the *main* subroutine in the pixel shader.

Unlike C and C++, the declarations at the top of a GLSL shader are within scope throughout the shader, even if the shader has multiple subroutines.

c) Determine if the pixel belongs to an odd or even row, and whether to an odd or even column. If row and column are both odd or both even, color black, else color white.

Bonuses

Bonus 1: make the upper half of the chessboard a checkerboard (i.e., black and red).

Bonus 2: produce a circular pattern, like below (should be about 7 lines of pixel shader).

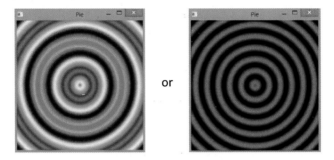

or

Figure 2-6: Circular patterns

Chapter 3: Ray-Tracing

Chapter 2 presented a simplified graphics pipeline that proceeds from object representation through to pixel shading; that is, the pipeline is *object-to-screen*. It is highly efficient and the most common method for real-time display of 2D and 3D geometry.

Before we develop our use of the pipeline in the following chapters, we reconsider the exercise from chapter two. The task was to produce a checkerboard by modifying the pixel shader. For each pixel, the shader determined which checkerboard square covered the pixel, rendering the image *screen-to-object*. Might the pixel shader compute a scene without the rasterizer processing individual scene elements?

Such an approach dates to the Renaissance, when artists developed techniques to draw with perspective. The grid method, seen below, is similar to computer *ray-tracing*.

Figure 3-1: Woodcut etching by Albrecht Dürer

In this chapter we develop a simple, animated ray-tracer, implemented almost entirely in the pixel shader. In the next chapter we return to the graphics pipeline.

3.1 Ray Geometry

To ray-trace, a ray is generated for each pixel of the display; the ray emanates from the camera (or "eye"), runs through the pixel, and is tested for intersection with objects in the scene. In the figure below, rays reflect off an object, then strike other objects, the background, or the light source.

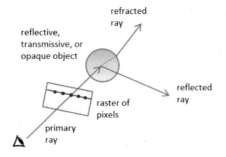

Figure 3-2: Primary ray through display and secondary rays

The first ray-traced image, below, demonstrates reflection, refraction, and shadows. These and other optical phenomena (e.g., caustics, glossiness, and atmospherics) are far more readily achieved with ray-tracing than with pipe-lined rasterization.

Figure 3-3: First ray-traced image by J. Turner Whitted
(used with permission)

Because adjacent rays can strike different objects, however, ray-tracing does not enjoy *pixel-to-pixel coherence*. Each ray intersection must be solved independently, and thus ray-tracing is much slower than rasterization (its relative efficiency does, however, improve as the processor/pixel ratio increases). For this reason, ray-tracing is usually reserved for special optical effects.

3.2 A Test Program

To demonstrate, let's develop a simple ray-tracing program that displays several spheres, one of which is highly reflective, against a backdrop of flat walls. The principal geometric operation will be to test whether a ray from the eye, through a given pixel, intersects a sphere or a wall.

21

Changes to the Vertex Shader

For most examples in this textbook, GLSL code is stored as a character string within the application source. This improves portability, and, usually, the vertex and pixel shaders don't unduly lengthen the application.

The pixel shader for this test program is sufficiently long to merit its own file; in the excerpt from RayTrace.cpp below, the pixel shader is read from the file RayTrace.glsl. Thus, the RayTrace.glsl can be changed without the need to recompile the application.

The vertex shader is written inline and relies on the built-in variable *gl_VertexID* to index one of the four vertices stored in the array, *pts*.

```
const char *quadVertexShader = "\
    #version 130
    vec2 pts[] = vec2[4](vec2(-1,-1), vec2(-1,1), vec2(1,1), vec2(1,-1));
    void main() {
        gl_Position = vec4(pts[gl_VertexID], 0, 1);
    }";
```

Changes to the Application

We can use the application from the previous chapter, with some modifications.

The inline vertex shader is compiled differently than the pixel shader, which is stored in a file. The two shaders are then linked into a program:

```
int v = CompileShaderViaCode(&quadVertexShader, GL_VERTEX_SHADER);
int p = CompileShaderViaFile("RayTrace.glsl", GL_FRAGMENT_SHADER);
program = LinkProgram(v, p);
```

The display subroutine draws a single quadrilateral, causing the hard-wired vertices to be fed to the rasterizer. These vertices (+/-1 in *X* and *Y*) are the corners of the default OpenGL display. Thus, as in the previous chapter (sec. 2.3), all the pixels in the display are shaded.

Animation

Because the display subroutine is called repeatedly by the event loop, we can animate the scene by changing the location of the spheres over time. In *Display*, the time elapsed since the beginning of program execution can control an angle of revolution (in this case, around the center of mass of all three spheres). This is applied to each sphere defined in RayTrace.cpp.

A sphere is a *vec4*, whose first three components (*.x*, *.y*, and *.z*) define its center and whose fourth, *.w*, defines the radius. In the following, *Display* updates the sphere centers and other *uniforms* (explained below) and calls *glDrawArrays*, causing an image to be ray-traced.

```
#include <time.h>
time_t start = clock();                          // app start time

void Display() {
    glUseProgram(program);
    // set window sizes, let viewPoint and viewDirection default
    SetUniform(program, "windowWidth", (float) winWidth);
    SetUniform(program, "windowHeight", (float) winHeight);
    // send planes, light to GPU
    SetUniform4v(program, "planes", 6, &planes[0].x);
    SetUniform(program, "light", light);
    vec4 ave = (spheres[0]+spheres[1]+spheres[2])/3;
    vec3 com(ave.x, ave.y, ave.z);               // center of mass
    // revolve spheres around center of mass
    float elapsed = (float)(clock()-start)/CLOCKS_PER_SEC;
    float a = 3.1415f*(-60.f*elapsed)/180.f; // 60 degrees/second
    float c = cos(a), s = sin(a);
    vec4 xSpheres[3];
    for (int i = 0; i < 3; i++) {
        // move origin to c.o.m., rotate, move back, set xSphere
        vec4 sph = spheres[i];
        vec3 q = vec3(sph.x, sph.y, sph.z)-com;
        vec3 xq = vec3(q.x*c-q.z*s, q.y, q.x*s+q.z*c)+com;
        xSpheres[i] = vec4(xq.x, xq.y, xq.z, sph.w);
    }
    // transfer 3 transformed spheres to shader, redraw
    SetUniform4v(program, "spheres", 3, &xSpheres[0].x);
    glDrawArrays(GL_QUADS, 0, 4);                // shade all pixels
    glFlush();
}
```

Uniforms

Because the program displays only spheres and planes, their intersections with a ray are readily calculated without intervening geometry (e.g., triangles). Thus, the application doesn't create a GPU vertex buffer or establish a vertex fetch.

The application communicates the camera location and view direction, the sphere and plane parameters, and light location to the GPU as uniforms.

Only basic types can be downloaded as a uniform; a *struct* cannot be used as a uniform input to a vertex shader.

The Ray-Primitive Intersection

To ray-trace each primitive type in a scene, it is necessary to compute the intersection of a ray with that primitive. For example, the ray/sphere intersection is derived below.

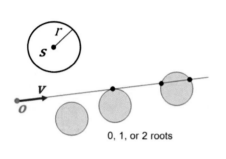

0, 1, or 2 roots

parametric ray: $p = o+tv$
implicit sphere: $|p-s|^2-r^2 = 0$

substituting for p
$$|o+tv-s|^2-r^2 = 0$$
dot product same as magnitude-squared
$$(o+tv-s)\bullet(o+tv-s)-r^2 = 0$$
substituting $q = o-s$
$$(tv+q)\bullet(tv+q)-r^2 = 0$$
expanding
$$t^2(v\bullet v)+2t(v\bullet q)+q\bullet q-r^2 = 0$$
assuming v is unit length
$$t^2+2t(v\bullet q)+q\bullet q-r^2 = 0$$
then apply quadratic formula with
$$a = 1,\ b = 2(v\bullet q),\ \text{and}\ c = q\bullet q-r^2$$

Figure 3-4: Calculation of ray/sphere intersection(s)

This readily converts to a GLSL subroutine, below, used by the pixel shader (the same subroutine is used to test for shadow in figure 1-9).

```
float RaySphere(Ray r, vec4 s) {
    // return least pos alpha intersect of ray/sphere (or -1 if none)
    vec3 q = r.b-s.xyz;
    float vDot = dot(r.v, q);
    float sq = vDot*vDot-dot(q, q)+s.w*s.w;
    if (sq < 0)
        return -1;
    float root = sqrt(sq), a = -vDot-root;
    if (a < 0)
        a = -vDot+root;
    return a >= 0? a : -1;
}
```

The Pixel Shader

The complete pixel shader and application are available online (see sec. 1.2); in this section we outline its functioning.

The pixel shader begins with uniform declarations that specify screen size, viewpoint and view direction; these are needed to determine the appropriate rays. Another uniform specifies a single light source. And three spheres and six planes are each represented as an array of 4D vectors. A 4D vector naturally describes a plane, and it also describes a sphere in terms of its 3D center and a radius.

A single output, an rgba color, is then declared.

'Built-in' GLSL variables are defined everywhere within the shader, and so the subroutine RayDirection is free to access gl_FragCoord (the coordinates of the pixel presently being shaded) and compute the direction from camera through pixel.

The pixel shader subroutines RaySphere and RayPlane compute ray intersections analytically, which is fast and accurate. One of the three spheres is considered reflective, so that should a ray strike it, it is reflected, using the GLSL function *reflect*.

GLSL features several functions useful to graphical computation, e.g., *log, min, max, sin, cos, abs, pow, asin, acos, log, sqrt, ceil, round, clamp,* cross and dot products, *reflect,* and *refract*.

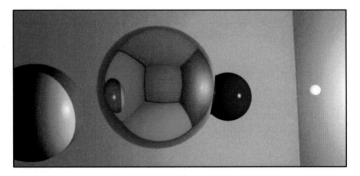

Figure 3-5: Image generated by RayTrace.glsl

The principal subroutines of the pixel shader include *RaySphere*, *RayPlane*, *InShadow*, and *Shade*. GLSL supports structures (but not as uniforms) and so the pixel shader defines a 'ray' structure that includes its base and direction.

The light source location is used to shade a pixel according to rules developed in chapter 9 and 10. The colors of the spheres and walls are defined as constants.

Ray-tracing excels at spheres, but with more intricate geometries its efficiency declines. And yet, it is often in demand for its ability to implement sophisticated optical effects. The pixel shader is isolated from the many practical concerns of the application, but, with ray-tracing, is capable of generating complex images.

3.3 Exercises

1. Modify the pixel shader so all spheres are reflective, and a ray may bounce up to five times.

2. Modify the pixel shader so that one sphere is translucent, and the ray refracts.

Chapter 4: Triangles

In chapter 3, spheres and planes were ray-traced without triangular approximations or vertex buffers. For more complex geometries, triangles (and quads) are usually preferred because of the inherent speed of rasterization. Triangles in particular are supported by numerous file formats and are a common exchange for geometric modeling, animation, rapid prototyping, and web browsing.

A *mesh* refers to a set of vertices and their connections to form *primitives*. Some meshes support *n*-sided polygons, but OpenGL is limited to triangles and quadrilaterals.

Modern shader architecture is designed to process a high volume of vertices, form primitives, rasterize them, and shade a high volume of pixels, all while granting the graphics programmer considerable access. The result is a more complex programming interface, which we describe in the next section.

4.1 Data and Control Paths

Consider the control and data paths between the CPU and GPU, diagrammed below for a typical OpenGL application.

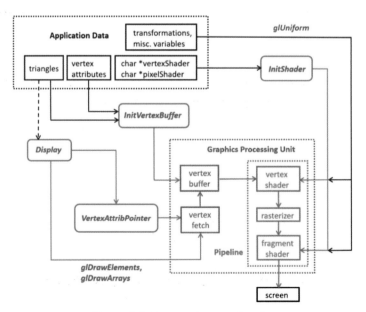

Figure 4-1: Data and control paths

Application data are in blue. Transformations and other variables can be controlled by the user and sent to the shaders via *glUniform* (sec. 3.2). The triangles (or quads) and vertices may be generated by the application or read from a file. GLSL shader code is read from a file or from within the application source, and sent to the shaders.

Paths to download vertices and control them are shown in green. The shader code is transferred to the GPU, compiled and linked within *InitShader*, and a vertex buffer is created and filled by the application in *InitVertexBuffer*.

Data from the vertex buffer must be connected to vertex shader inputs, which is arranged with calls to *VertexAttribPointer*. Vertex attributes typically include surface position, color, surface direction (the *surface normal*), and texture (*uv coordinates*).

Finally, the *Display* subroutine calls *glDrawArrays* or *glDrawElements*, causing attributes from the vertex buffer to be fed to the vertex shader. This begins the pipeline process, shown in red.

4.2 Rasterization

Vertex triplets (i.e., triangles) are distributed across GPU processors, each executing the vertex shader. The shader transforms each vertex by a given view and passes the transformed locations (and any other vertex attributes enabled by *VertexAttribPointer*) to the rasterizer.

For a triangle (v_1, v_2, v_3), the rasterizer receives the display location and other attributes for each of the three vertices. These attribute values are interpolated from the three triangle corners using *forward differencing* (a form of *recurrence*).

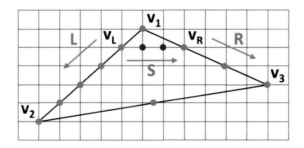

Figure 4-2: Bilinear interpolation during rasterization

28

Referring to figure 4-2, consider a vertex attribute, say color, interpolated down the left and right edges, one scan line (i.e., row) at a time.

Along the left edge are six scan lines from v_1 to v_2, so each line spans 1/5 of the color change from v_1 to v_2; i.e., $dColorL = (color_2-color_1)/5$. Similarly, $dColorR = (color_3-color_1)/3$. The color at v_L is thus $color_L = color_1+dColorL$, and similarly for v_R. Forward differencing can now be applied between v_L and v_R to compute the inner, blue pixel values.

The result is a *bilinear interpolation* of vertex attributes across those pixels covered by triangle $v_1v_2v_3$. The interpolation is achieved mostly through addition, which accounts for its speed. The results are said to have *pixel-to-pixel coherence*, that is, adjacent pixels have similar values.

This method of rasterization has been fundamental to OpenGL. Attributes can include position in perspective space (i.e., *gl_Position*), position on the surface, surface normal, color, and texture.

4.3 A Colorful Triangle

A colorful triangle provides a good example of rasterization. It requires half a dozen changes to ClearScreen.cpp:

1. The application defines three points (not four) and an array of three colors
2. The vertex shader defines a new input "color" and a new output "vColor"
3. The pixel shader defines a new input "vColor" and a new output "pColor"
4. The pixel shader output is set to its input (the color produced by the rasterizer)
5. The display subroutine clears the screen to white, and
6. *glDrawArrays* is called with GL_TRIANGLES (not QUADS) and 3 (not 4) vertices.

Figure 4-3: Rendered triangle

The complete program is given below. To prevent memory leaks, the vertex buffer is freed on exit from the event loop.

```cpp
// ColorfulTriangle.cpp: draw triangle via GLSL and vertex buffer

#include <glad.h>
#include <GLFW/glfw3.h>
#include <stdio.h>
#include "GLXtras.h"

// GPU identifiers
GLuint vBuffer = 0;
GLuint program = 0;

// a triangle (3 2D locations, 3 RGB colors)
float points[][2] = {{-.45f, -.45f}, {.1f, .45f}, {.75f, 0}};
float colors[][3] = {{1, 0, 0}, {0, 1, 0}, {0, 0, 1}};  // change #1

const char *vertexShader = "\
    #version 150
    in vec2 point;
    in vec3 color;                                        // change #2
    out vec4 vColor;
    void main() {
        gl_Position = vec4(point, 0, 1);
        vColor = vec4(color, 1);
    }";

const char *pixelShader = "\
    #version 150
    in vec4 vColor;
    out vec4 pColor;                                      // change #3
    void main() {
        pColor = vColor;                                  // change #4
    }";

void InitVertexBuffer() {
    // make GPU buffer for points & colors, set it active buffer
    glGenBuffers(1, &vBuffer);
    glBindBuffer(GL_ARRAY_BUFFER, vBuffer);
    // allocate buffer memory to hold points and colors
    int sPnts = sizeof(points), sCols = sizeof(colors);
    glBufferData(GL_ARRAY_BUFFER, sPnts+sCols, NULL, GL_STATIC_DRAW);
    // load data to the GPU
    glBufferSubData(GL_ARRAY_BUFFER, 0, sPnts, points);
        // start at start of buffer, for length of points array
    glBufferSubData(GL_ARRAY_BUFFER, sPnts, sCols, colors);
        // start at end of points array, for length of colors
}
```

```
void Display() {
    glClearColor(1,1,1,1);
    glClear(GL_COLOR_BUFFER_BIT);                           // change #5
    // access GPU vertex buffer
    glUseProgram(program);
    glBindBuffer(GL_ARRAY_BUFFER, vBuffer);
    // connect vertex buffer to position input of vertex shader
    VertexAttribPointer(program, "point", 2, 0, (void *) 0);
    // connect color in vertex buffer to input vertex buffer
    VertexAttribPointer(program, "color", 3, 0, (void *) sizeof(points));
    // render three vertices as a triangle
    glDrawArrays(GL_TRIANGLES, 0, 3);                       // change #6
    glFlush();
}

int main() {
    if (!glfwInit())
        return 1;
    GLFWwindow *w = glfwCreateWindow(600, 600, "Triangle", NULL, NULL);
    if (!w) {
        glfwTerminate();
        return 1;
    }
    glfwMakeContextCurrent(w);
    gladLoadGLLoader((GLADloadproc) glfwGetProcAddress);
    printf("GL version: %s\n", glGetString(GL_VERSION));
    PrintGLErrors();
    program = LinkProgramViaCode(&vertexShader, &pixelShader);
    if (!program)
        return 0;
    InitVertexBuffer();
    while (!glfwWindowShouldClose(w)) {
        Display();
        glfwSwapBuffers(w);
        glfwPollEvents();
    }
    // unbind vertex buffer, free GPU memory
    glBindBuffer(GL_ARRAY_BUFFER, 0);
    glDeleteBuffers(1, &vBuffer);
    glfwDestroyWindow(w);
    glfwTerminate();
}
```

4.4 Colorful Triangles

To represent and display multiple triangles, a natural extension to ColorfulTriangle is an increase in the number of points and colors. For example, below are 10 vertices that form 9 triangles, and the resulting shaded image.

31

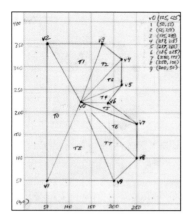 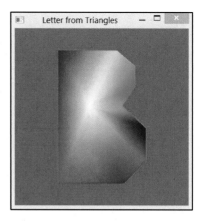

Figure 4-4: Design and rendering of a colorful letter

OpenGL offers two methods to send these vertices to the vertex shader.

DrawArrays vs. DrawElements

In ColorfulTriangle.cpp the call to *DrawArrays* causes three vertices to be poured from GPU memory into the vertex shader. In the case of the 'B', a total of 9 triangles implies 27 vertices must populate the vertex buffer (i.e., the center would appear 9 times in the array, and each of the perimeter vertices would appear twice), rather than the original 10 vertices. The process of converting 9 triangles to 27 vertices in the GPU buffer accounts for the connection in figure 4.1 between *triangles* and *InitVertexBuffer*.

As an alternative to *DrawArrays*, the *DrawElements* method requires only unique vertices in GPU memory, that is, the original 10. The same 27 vertices must be fed to the vertex shader, but they are obtained from the original 10 indirectly via an array of 27 integer indices.

These indices are readily created on inspection for the 'B'; the center vertex with index 0 appears nine times; the other indices each appear twice.

```
int triangles[][3] = {
  {0,1,2},{0,2,3},{0,3,4},{0,4,5},{0,5,6},{0,6,7},{0,7,8},{0,8,9},{0,9,1}
};
```

DrawElements requires a pointer to this triangle array, which accounts for the dashed line connecting *triangles* to the *Display* subroutine in figure 4.1.

32

4.5 Exercise: A Colorful Letter

The objective of this exercise is to modify ColorfulTriangle to display multiple triangles. This can be done with the following steps:

Step 1) Rename a copy of ColorfulTriangle.cpp to ColorfulLetter.cpp.

Step 2) Pick a letter of the alphabet, draw its outline on graph paper, divide it into two or more triangles, label the vertices, and connect them to form the triangles.

Step 3) Measure the vertex coordinates, in X and Y. Center and/or scale the coordinates to be in a +/- 1 range (the default OpenGL display range).

Step 4) In ColorfulLetter, change the "// a triangle" comment to "// vertices" and

   a) resize the points array to correspond with your letter
   b) resize the colors array to correspond with the points array.

Step 5) After the vertices, add an array of triangles:

   a) add a // "triangles" comment
   b) for each triangle triplet (a, b, c), create an entry {aID, bID, cID} in the array; e.g.,

```
int triangles[][3] = {{0, 1, 2}, {1, 2, 3} ... };
```

Step 6) In *Display*, call *glDrawElements*, not *glDrawArrays*; change 27 to the actual number of vertices), passing a pointer to the triangle indices:

```
glDrawElements(GL_TRIANGLES, 27, GL_UNSIGNED_INT, triangles);
```

Step 7) Check

   a) the letter should look like the one you graphed
   b) all the vertices should be colored
   c) the colors should be continuous (smooth) at the vertices

Contiguous vs. Interleaved Vertex Attributes

In ColorfulTriangle.cpp and ColorfulLetter.cpp the vertex locations ("points") and the vertex colors are stored as adjacent but separate, contiguous arrays in the GPU vertex buffer. That is, the GPU buffer looks like:

point[0]	point[1]	point[2]	color[0]	color[1]	color[2]

Figure 4-5: Adjacent arrays

For applications that have numerous vertex attributes, it can be advantageous to store attributes interleaved, so that entire vertices appear in sequence. That is, the GPU buffer would look like:

point[0]	color[0]	point[1]	color[1]	point[2]	color[2]

Figure 4-6: Interleaved arrays

This is readily achieved with a structure:

```
struct Vertex {
  vec2 point;
  vec3 color;
  Vertex(float x, float y, float r, float g, float b) :
      point(x,y), color(r,g,b) { }
};
```

The 'B' can be represented by 10 vertices, each with an *x,y* location and an *r,g,b* color:

```
Vertex vertices[] = {
    Vertex(-.15f, .125f,  1,  1, 1), Vertex(-.5f,  -.75f,  1,  0,  0),
    Vertex(-.5f,   .75f, .5f, 0, 0), Vertex( .17f,  .75f,  1,  1,  0),
    Vertex( .38f, .575f, .5f, 1, 0), Vertex( .38f,  .35f,  0,  1,  0),
    Vertex( .23f, .125f,  0,  1, 1), Vertex( .5f,  -.125f, 0,  0,  1),
    Vertex( .5f,  -.5f,   1,  0, 1), Vertex( .25f, -.75f, .5f, 0, .5f)
};
```

In *InitVertexBuffer*, copying the vertices to the GPU becomes simpler: rather than one call to *glBufferData* and two calls to *glBufferSubData*, we need only a single call:

```
glBufferData(GL_ARRAY_BUFFER, sizeof(vertices), vertices, GL_STATIC_DRAW);
```

The calls in *Display* to *VertexAttribPointer* must change in two ways.

The *stride* argument indicates the distance (number of bytes) in memory between sequential vertex attributes. When using contiguous arrays, two sequential colors (for example) are adjacent to each other in memory and thus their stride is 0. But the stride of interleaved attributes is, in the present instance, `sizeof`(Vertex).

The *offset* (last) argument remains 0 for the point attribute, but for the color attribute it is no longer the length of the points array, but rather the length of a single point. Thus, the two calls to *VertexAttribPointer* become:

```
VertexAttribPointer(program, "point", 2, sizeof(Vertex), (void *) 0);
VertexAttribPointer(program, "color", 3, sizeof(Vertex), (void *) sizeof(vec2));
            // shader      name  dim      stride          offset
```

This arrangement of subroutine arguments allow flexible access to GPU memory, but the programmer must take care as many bugs originate with these calls.

Bonus 1: Interleaved

Modify your solution to exercise 4.5 to use interleaved attributes.

Bonus 2: Alternating Triangles

Modify *Display* so that it draws colors every other triangle, with the alternate triangles having a flat shade. The following code offers a hint.

```
int ntriangles = sizeof(triangles)/3;
for (int i = 0; i < ntriangles; i ++)
    glDrawElements(GL_TRIANGLES, 3, GL_UNSIGNED_INT, triangles[i]);
```

This accomplishes exactly the same as the single call (but one triangle at a time):

```
glDrawElements(GL_TRIANGLES, sizeof(triangles), GL_UNSIGNED_INT, triangles);
```

A uniform variable in the pixel shader can control the type of shading (flat or colorful).

An alternative is to create a second shader program that only flat shades (i.e., define a second pixel shader that sets its pixel output to a fixed color). Then, call *glUseProgram* for the first program and colorfully shade the odd-numbered triangles; then call *glUseProgram* for the second program and flat shade the even-numbered triangles.

Chapter 5: Geometric Transformations

In our previous examples, the vertex shader has had little to do. In this chapter we consider its use to transform the location of an input vertex. We first examine the basic two-dimensional transformations of scale, translation, and rotation.

5.1 Scale and Translation of a Point

A given point (x, y) can be scaled by a factor s to produce a scaled point:

$(x', y') = (sx, sy)$.

A given point (x, y) can be translated (moved in a straight line) a distance (dx, dy):

$(x', y') = (x+dx, y+dy)$.

5.2 Rotation of a Point

Rotation is not as obvious as scale or translation. The easiest development is via the *angle sum identities*:

(5.1) $\cos(\alpha+\beta) = \cos(\alpha)\cos(\beta) - \sin(\alpha)\sin(\beta)$

$\sin(\alpha+\beta) = \sin(\alpha)\cos(\beta) + \cos(\alpha)\sin(\beta)$

These identities were discovered by 10th century mathematician and astronomer, Abu al-Wafa Buzjani.

Figure 5-1: Abu al-Wafa Buzjani

Consider a point (x, y) in the XY plane and its rotation counter-clockwise about the origin by the amount β radians.

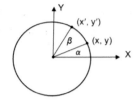

Figure 5-2: Rotation of (x, y)

For convenience, let's assume (x, y) is on the unit circle (the results will hold for any radius). Thus, the point (x, y) is $(\cos α, \sin α)$ and the rotated point (x', y') is $(\cos(α+β), \sin(α+β))$. Applying the angle sum identities, we can give x' and y' in terms of x, y, and β.

(5.2) $x' = \cos(α+β) = \cos α \cos β - \sin α \sin β = x \cos β - y \sin β$
          $y' = \sin(α+β) = \sin α \cos β + \cos α \sin β = y \cos β + x \sin β$

Rotation about an Arbitrary Center

The above rotation has the origin as its center. To produce a rotation about an arbitrary center c, we shift the coordinate system to c, rotate, and then shift back:

(5.3) $x' = c_x+(x-c_x) \cos ß - (y-c_y) \sin ß$
          $y' = c_y+(x-c_x) \sin ß + (y-c_y) \cos ß$

5.3 Exercise: A Rotating Letter

In this exercise we modify 'colorful letter' to become 'rotating colorful letter'. It will be convenient to represent points as a vector, i.e., (x,y) is of type *vec2*, (x,y,z) of type *vec3*, etc. These types are defined in VecMat.h, requiring an include statement.

We define a rotation angle β, update it in the event loop based on the application's elapsed time, and send it to the vertex shader as a uniform. In the vertex shader, GLSL's *sin* and *cos* are used to rotate incoming points according to equation 5.2.

Changes to Vertex Shader

No change is needed to the pixel shader, but the vertex shader must rotate incoming vertices by a given angle. This is declared before *main* in the vertex shader:

```
uniform float ang = 0;          // rotation in radians
```

The vertices passed to the vertex shader are rotated by a subroutine that should follow the uniform declaration. (Unlike C syntax, the uniform *ang* is within scope of the body of *Rotate2D*):

```
vec2 Rotate2D(vec2 v) {
    // return v rotated about origin by ang
    return vec2( ... );
}
```

Finally, in the *main* subroutine of the vertex shader, the assignment to *gl_Position* becomes:

```
vec2 r = Rotate2D(point);
gl_Position = vec4(r, 0, 1);
```

Event Loop Animation

Animation is achieved by the event loop of the application. Each iteration calls *Display*, which sets the rotation angle based on time elapsed during the application's execution. This should produce a smoothly rotating object.

To determine the time elapsed since the last call, a reference time is declared and initialized as a global variable. A rotational speed is also given:

```
time_t startTime = clock();
static float degPerSec = 30;

void Display() {
    // compute elapsed time, determine radAng, send to GPU
    float dt = (float)(clock()-startTime)/CLOCKS_PER_SEC
    SetUniform(program, "radAng", (3.1415f/180.f)*dt*degPerSec);
    // clear to gray, use app's shader
    glClearColor(.5, .5, .5, 1);
    glClear(GL_COLOR_BUFFER_BIT);
    glUseProgram(program);
    // set vertex feed for points and colors, then draw
    VertexAttribPointer(program, "point", 2, 0, (void *) 0);
    VertexAttribPointer(program, "color", 3, 0, (void *) sizeof(points));
    int nvertices = sizeof(triangles)/sizeof(int);
    glDrawElements(GL_TRIANGLES, nvertices, GL_UNSIGNED_INT, triangles);
    glFlush();
}
```

Coding Hint: Verify Shaders Work

The software in this exercise is relatively simple and not prone to error. But when more complex methods are used, it can be useful to suspend the animation in order to ensure there are no run-time GLSL problems (*e.g.*, shader input naming errors). This is because, once the animation runs, additional errors may be continuously written to the console, obscuring any initial GLSL errors. Alternatively, if the application uses error handlers, a call to *getchar* in each will pause the console output.

Bonus 1: Scale

In addition to rotation, apply a *scale* that changes over time.

Bonus 2: Speed Control

We can control the rotation speed with the keyboard, so it will increase ('A'), decrease ("D"), reverse ("R"), or reset ("S") by registering a callback in the application's *main*:

```
glfwSetKeyCallback(window, Keyboard);
```

Once registered, the following subroutine is called whenever the user types a key.

```
void Keyboard(GLFWwindow *w, int key, int code, int action, int mods) {
    // speed up, down or reverse rotation
    switch (key) {
        case 'A': degPerSec *= 1.3f;                        break; // fast
        case 'S': degPerSec = degPerSec < 0? -30 : 30; break; // reset
        case 'D': degPerSec *= .7f;                         break; // slow
        case 'R': degPerSec *= -1;                          break; // rev
    }
}
```

Bonus 3: Improved Speed Control

In bonus 2, there is a sudden jump in the angle whenever *degPerSec* is changed; implement code to prevent this.

Chapter 6: Matrices

In the previous exercise we sent an angle to the vertex shader, where it was used to rotate input vertices. It is in the vertex shader that vertices are efficiently transformed from their defining coordinate system to that of the display. In this chapter we examine some basic, geometric transformations performed by the vertex shader.

We also examine a *matrix* of four rows and four columns, which can represent any combination of these transformations. For this reason, a matrix, rather than an individual parameter (e.g., *ang* in sec. 5.3), is provided to the vertex shader.

The dimension of a matrix refers to the number of its rows and columns, given as *n by m* (*n* rows and *m* columns), usually abbreviated *n X m*.

To represent and operate on a matrix, we use *mat4*, defined in VecMat.h. A brief summary of vector algebra and matrix operations is found at the end of this chapter.

6.1 The Matrix as a Geometric Transformation

In the 1960s, Larry Roberts introduced matrices to his work in computer vision and computer graphics. He noted, "The interpretation of a matrix as a geometrical operator is the foundation of mathematical transformations useful in computer graphics."

Figure 6-1: Larry Roberts

Rotation and Scale

Let's reconsider the rotation equations from the previous chapter:

(6-1) $x' = x \cos \theta - y \sin \theta$
$y' = x \sin \theta + y \cos \theta$

This is a *linear system*: it is a system because two input variables yield two output values; it is linear because the equations perform only linear operations (as opposed to, say, exponentiation) on an input variable.

The system is readily represented as a 2 X 2 matrix because multiplication of a matrix by a 2D vector obeys the following rule:

(6-2)
$$\begin{bmatrix} x' \\ y' \end{bmatrix} = \begin{bmatrix} a & b \\ c & d \end{bmatrix} \begin{bmatrix} x \\ y \end{bmatrix} = \begin{bmatrix} ax + by \\ cx + dy \end{bmatrix}$$

Applying (6-2), the algebraic equations in (6-1) are represented in matrix form by:

(6-3)
$$\begin{bmatrix} x' \\ y' \end{bmatrix} = \begin{bmatrix} \cos\theta & -\sin\theta \\ \sin\theta & \cos\theta \end{bmatrix} \begin{bmatrix} x \\ y \end{bmatrix}$$

Similarly, the algebraic and matrix forms for scale are:

Algebraic form	Matrix form
$x' = s_x x$ $y' = s_y y$	$\begin{bmatrix} x' \\ y' \end{bmatrix} = \begin{bmatrix} s_x & 0 \\ 0 & s_y \end{bmatrix} \begin{bmatrix} x \\ y \end{bmatrix}$

When $s_x = s_y$, the scale is *uniform*, otherwise it is *differential*.

Translation

Equation (6-2) can be understood as a component-wise *dot product* of the input vector and the corresponding row of the matrix. Because the result is a linear combination of the input x and y, it cannot be offset by a constant. That is, equation (6-2) does not permit *translation* (straight-line motion).

To accommodate translation, we add a column to the matrix for the translation components. Because the multiplication requires the vector dimension be equal to the number of matrix columns, we also add a *homogeneous coordinate* (defaulting to 1) to the vector (x, y):

41

Algebraic form	Matrix form

$$\begin{aligned} x' &= x + t_x \\ y' &= y + t_y \end{aligned} \qquad \begin{bmatrix} x' \\ y' \end{bmatrix} = \begin{bmatrix} 1 & 0 & t_x \\ 0 & 1 & t_y \end{bmatrix} \begin{bmatrix} x \\ y \\ 1 \end{bmatrix}$$

We compute x' by multiplying the first row of the matrix with the input vector:

$(1, 0, t_x) \bullet (x, y, 1) = 1(x) + 0(y) + 1(t_x) = x + t_x.$

The translation results from the *addition* in the dot product, but it is disguised as a matrix *multiplication*. (Incidentally, because the matrix can now produce translation, it is no longer said to be linear, but *affine*).

Compared with the above 2 X 3 matrix, a *square*, 3 X 3 matrix is preferred because:

- only a square matrix is invertible
- a vector multiplied by a square matrix yields a vector of the same dimension
- square matrices, when multiplied, yield a square matrix

Thus, an extra row is also added to the matrix:

$$\begin{bmatrix} x' \\ y' \\ w' \end{bmatrix} = \begin{bmatrix} 1 & 0 & tx \\ 0 & 1 & ty \\ 0 & 0 & 1 \end{bmatrix} \begin{bmatrix} x \\ y \\ 1 \end{bmatrix}$$

This multiplication yields the same x' and y' result, and an additional *homogeneous coordinate*, w (in this case, equal to 1).

6.2 The Homogeneous Coordinate

"Homogeneous" signifies all terms in an equation are of the same degree, which is true if the above translation treats *x*, *y*, and *w* as variables. In this way, homogeneous coordinates enable translation to be treated in the same manner as scale and rotation. (They have an important additional use, described in the next chapter.)

The homogeneous coordinate system is one in which *n+1* values represent an *n*-dimensional point. They were introduced in 1827 by Möbius who defined a 2D point within a triangle as a weighted sum of the triangle vertices: the three coefficients expressed the point in a 'barycentric coordinate' homogeneous system.

Homogeneous coordinates have a natural application to computer graphics, ever since their use by Roberts in 1963. As we will see, they can represent points at infinity with finite coordinates, and formulas are more compact and consistent than when expressed in Cartesian coordinates.

6.3 The 4 X 4 Matrix

The above scale, rotation, and translation matrices were developed for two-dimensional points. The matrices are readily extended to three dimensions.

For example, two-dimensional rotation is the same as three-dimensional rotation in the *XY* plane, i.e., rotation about the *Z*-axis. The *z*-coordinate is accommodated by adding an extra row and extra column to produce a 4 X 4 matrix. It yields the same transformations to *x* and *y* while the *z*-coordinate is unchanged.

$$[x \cos\theta - y \sin\theta , x \sin\theta + y \cos\theta, 0, 1] = \begin{bmatrix} \cos\theta & -\sin\theta & 0 & 0 \\ \sin\theta & \cos\theta & 0 & 0 \\ 0 & 0 & 1 & 0 \\ 0 & 0 & 0 & 1 \end{bmatrix} \begin{bmatrix} x \\ y \\ z \\ 1 \end{bmatrix}$$

z-rotation

Here are the 4 X 4 matrix representations for the most common geometric transformations.

$$\begin{bmatrix} S_x & 0 & 0 & 0 \\ 0 & S_y & 0 & 0 \\ 0 & 0 & S_z & 0 \\ 0 & 0 & 0 & 1 \end{bmatrix} \qquad \begin{bmatrix} 1 & 0 & 0 & t_x \\ 0 & 1 & 0 & t_y \\ 0 & 0 & 1 & t_z \\ 0 & 0 & 0 & 1 \end{bmatrix}$$

scale   *translation*

Although scale and translation in 3D simply require an additional row and column, rotation in 3D must contend with three rotation axes. Their corresponding matrices are below. θ is in radians.

$$\begin{bmatrix} 1 & 0 & 0 & 0 \\ 0 & \cos\theta & -\sin\theta & 0 \\ 0 & \sin\theta & \cos\theta & 0 \\ 0 & 0 & 0 & 1 \end{bmatrix} \quad \begin{bmatrix} \cos\theta & 0 & \sin\theta & 0 \\ 0 & 1 & 0 & 0 \\ -\sin\theta & 0 & \cos\theta & 0 \\ 0 & 0 & 0 & 1 \end{bmatrix} \quad \begin{bmatrix} \cos\theta & -\sin\theta & 0 & 0 \\ \sin\theta & \cos\theta & 0 & 0 \\ 0 & 0 & 1 & 0 \\ 0 & 0 & 0 & 1 \end{bmatrix}$$

rotation about X-axis *rotation about Y-axis* *rotation about Z-axis*

Vector and Matrix Types

VecMat.h is found on the text website; it is a header file that defines *mat4*, a 4 X 4 matrix class, as well as *vec2*, *vec3*, and *vec4* vector classes. The same types are defined in GLSL.

VecMat.h implements the above transformations with the following subroutines:

```
mat4 m = Scale(sx, sy, sz);
mat4 m = Translate(tx, ty, tz);
mat4 m = RotateX(α);    // (α in degrees)
mat4 m = RotateY(α);
mat4 m = RotateZ(α);
```

A transformation can be applied to an ordinary 3D point vec3 *p(x, y, z)* if *p* is first promoted to a homogeneous point and then pre-multiplied by the transformation matrix, yielding a transformed homogeneous point *xp*:

```
vec4 xp = m*vec4(p,1);
```

Conventions

In order that *z*-depth increase into the screen, early graphics development used a left-handed coordinate system, and points represented as row vectors were post-multiplied by matrices.

Modern texts develop computer graphics with a traditional right-handed coordinate system in which the perspective-space z-axis points out from the screen and column vectors are pre-multiplied by matrices (as in the previous section). OpenGL and GLSL subscribe to these conventions.

Rotations subscribe to the right-hand rule in which the right thumb points along an axis and the fingers curl in the direction of positive rotation.

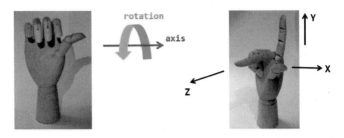

Figure 6-2: Right-handed rotation and right-handed coordinate system

Storage of a matrix in memory is called *row-major order* if the first four elements in memory are its first row, namely m[0][0], m[0][1], m[0][2], and m[0][3]; the matrix is *column-major order* if its first four elements form the first column, namely m[0][0], m[1][0], m[2][0], and m[3][0].

OpenGL and VecMat.h subroutines expect a column-major matrix, i.e., a series of 16 floats as described above. Some OpenGL subroutines provide an option to *transpose* the matrix, which converts between row and column order.

Concatenations

Multiple transformations, *e.g.*, [T][S][Rₓ][Rᵧ][Rᵤ], can be *concatenated* into a single, mathematically equivalent, matrix. This is simple to express given the operator overloading in VecMat.h. For example:

```
mat4 xform = Translate(dx,dy,dz)*RotateZ(30)*RotateY(15);
    // rotate about Y, then about Z, then translate
```

In text, we write m1m2 to suggest two matrices are multiplied in left-to-right order. In C++, however, we code from right-to-left. (This is a consequence of the matrix layout in memory and the fact that column vectors are pre-multiplied by matrices).

Therefore, if a 3D point (*x, y, z*) is to be transformed first by **m₁** and then by **m₂**, it would be coded as:

```
vec4 p(x,y,z,1);
vec4 q = m2*m1*p;
```

Or:

```
mat4 m = m2*m1;
vec4 q = m*p;
```

The resulting 3D point is ($q.x$, $q.y$, $q.z$).

6.4 Transformation Order

The *concatenation* of 3D scale, rotation, and translation matrices, any combination in any order, yields a single 4 X 4 matrix representing a continuous, affine transformation. The geometric meaning depends on the order of transformations. In particular, very different orientations and locations can result when transformations are re-ordered.

Effect of Rotation / Translation Order

Consider a point, a rotation, and a translation in two dimensions:

```
vec4 p(1, 0, 0, 1);          // same as 2D point in XY-plane
mat4 R = RotateZ(90);        // rotation in XY-plane
mat4 T = Translate(-1, -1, 0);  // translation in XY-plane
```

If *p* is first rotated (blue arrow), it becomes (0,1) and then, when translated (green), becomes (-1, 0).

```
vec4 xp = Translate(-1,-1,0)*RotateZ(90)*p
```

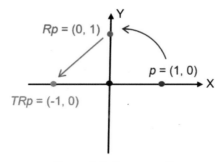

Figure 6-3: Sequence 1

46

If, however, p is translated (blue arrow), it becomes (0, -1) and then, when rotated (green), returns to (1, 0).

```
vec4 xp = RotateZ(90)*Translate(-1,-1,0)*p;
```

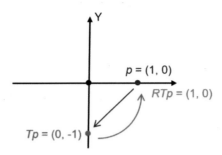

Figure 6-4: Sequence 2

Effect of Rotation / Rotation Order

In two dimensions, a series of rotations may be re-ordered because the combination amounts to a summation of the rotation angles. This is not the case in three dimensions because there are multiple axes of rotation.

For example, consider these two rotations:

```
mat4 R1 = RotateX(90);
mat4 R2 = RotateY(90);
```

A point p can undergo two possible transformations:

```
vec4 xp1 = R1*R2*p;     // rotate about Y-axis, then X
vec4 xp2 = R2*R1*p;     // rotate about X-axis, then Y
```

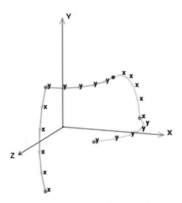

Figure 6-5: Rotation Order

47

The path of *xp1* is shown in cyan, beginning at the blue dot. First is the rotation around the Y-axis (shown as a series of 'y's ending at a green dot), then around the X-axis (shown as 'x's ending at a red dot). The path of *xp2* is shown in orange and yields a different result.

6.5 Matrix Use in the Vertex Shader

In the previous exercise, we passed *radAng* to the vertex shader:

```
in vec2 point;
uniform float radAng = 0;
vec2 Rotate2D(vec2 v) {
     float c = cos(radAng), s = sin(radAng);
     return vec2(c*v.x-s*v.y, s*v.x+c*v.y);
}
void main() {
     vec2 r = Rotate2D(point);
     gl_Position = vec4(r, 0, 1);
}
```

If the application uses a matrix, the shader becomes simpler and more general:

```
in vec2 point;
uniform mat4 view;
void main() {
     gl_Position = view*vec4(point, 0, 1);
}
```

The 2D input point is promoted to 4D (with a *z* value of 0 and homogeneous value of 1).

The application computes a matrix given a rotation angle and passes it to the vertex shader. This can be done in *Display*:

```
mat4 xform = RotateZ(radAng);
SetUniform(program, "view", xform);
```

The use of a 4 X 4 matrix allows *Display* to send, in a standard form, any *affine* or (as we'll see in the next chapter) *projective* transformation to the vertex shader.

gl_Position

A primary responsibility of the vertex shader is to set the homogeneous point gl_*Position*. We will consider gl_*Position* and homogeneous coordinates further in the next chapter.

6.6 Exercise: Rotate3DLetter

Let's modify the exercise from the previous chapter so that

a) the letter rotates in response to user input,
b) the letter rotates in three dimensions, and
c) a matrix is used for transformations

The previous exercise rotated vertices in the *XY* plane (i.e., rotation about the *Z*-axis). In this exercise, we'll rotate vertices about the *X* and *Y* axes, with the extent of rotation dependent on the amount the user drags the mouse. The resulting transformed letter will no longer be parallel with the screen. It will appear to rotate in three dimensions.

Mouse Interaction

To control *X* and *Y* rotations with the mouse, we need several new variables, a callback to handle mouse buttons, and a callback to handle mouse movement.

A) New Variables

In order to maintain rotational continuity between mouse clicks, we define the following global variables:

```
vec2 mouseDown(0,0);          // location of last mouse down
vec2 rotOld(0,0), rotNew(0,0);   // .x is rotation about Y-axis, in degrees; .y about X-axis
```

As the rotation will be user-driven, we replace the *degPerSec* variable of the previous exercise with this generic speed factor:

```
float rotSpeed = .3f;         // degree rotation per #pixels dragged by mouse
```

B) Button Callback

The following callback is needed to respond to mouse clicks.

```
void MouseButton(GLFWwindow *w, int butn, int action, int mods) {
    // called when mouse button pressed or released
    if (action == GLFW_PRESS) {
        // save reference for MouseDrag
        double x, y;
        glfwGetCursorPos(w, &x, &y);
        mouseDown = vec2((float) x, (float) y);
    }
    if (action == GLFW_RELEASE)
        // save reference rotation
        rotOld = rotNew;
}
```

This callback is registered in *main* with:

```
glfwSetMouseButtonCallback(window, MouseButton);
```

C) Motion (Drag) Callback

The following callback is needed to respond to mouse movement:

```
void MouseMove(GLFWwindow *w, double x, double y) {
    if (glfwGetMouseButton(w, GLFW_MOUSE_BUTTON_LEFT) == GLFW_PRESS) {
        // compute mouse drag difference, update rotation
        vec2 dif((float)x-mouseDown.x, (float)y-mouseDown.y);
        rotNew = rotOld+rotSpeed*dif;
    }
}
```

This callback modifies the *x* and *y* rotation values based on the amount the mouse is dragged after it is clicked down. It is registered with *glfwSetCursorPosCallback*.

Euler Angles

The rotation matrices given in section 6.3 define separate rotations around the *X*, *Y*, and *Z* axes. In combination these can produce a rotation about any axis. Collectively they are called *Euler angles*, for the 18th century Swiss mathematician and physicist Leonhard Euler. If a plane were flying parallel with the *x*-axis, with the *z*-axis up, we might say that rotation about the *y*-axis is *pitch*, rotation about the *z*-axis is *yaw*, and rotation about the *x*-axis is *roll*.

Euler angles are easily implemented and provide the user basic control of an object's orientation. They are not always intuitive to use, however, and are subject to *gimbal lock*, in which combinations of angles severely constrain subsequent rotations.

In a later chapter we consider issues of orientation within a tree of transformations, and how the issues of gimbal lock and interpolation of reference frames motivate the use of *quaternions*.

Changes to Display

Before drawing any triangles, *Display* must compute the transformation matrix using routines in VecMat.h. It then updates the matrix shader uniform.

```
mat4 view = RotateY(rotNew.x)*RotateX(rotNew.y);
SetUniform(program, "view", view);
```

Bonus 1: Move

For this bonus, we wish the mouse to control translation (move) if the SHIFT key is held; otherwise the mouse controls rotation.

As with *rotOld*, *rotNew*, and *rotSpeed*, we need a set of variables to control translation:

```
vec2 tranOld(0,0), tranNew(0,0);
float tranSpeed = .01f;
```

MouseButton must be modified:

```
if (action == GLFW_RELEASE) {
    rotOld = rotNew;
    tranOld = tranNew;
}
```

And *MouseDrag* must be modified:

```
vec2 mouse((float) x, (float) y), dif = mouse-mouseDown;
bool shift = glfwGetKey(w, GLFW_KEY_LEFT_SHIFT) == GLFW_PRESS ||
            glfwGetKey(w, GLFW_KEY_RIGHT_SHIFT) == GLFW_PRESS;
// translate or rotate
if (shift)
        tranNew = tranOld+tranSpeed*vec2(dif.x, -dif.y);
    else
        rotNew = rotOld+rotSpeed*dif;
```

Finally, *Display* should include the translation as part of the matrix concatenation:

mat4 m = Translate(tranNew.x,tranNew.y,0)*RotateY(rotNew.x)*RotateX(rotNew.y);

SetUniform(program, "view", m);

Bonus 2: Roll

Use the mouse wheel to control *Z* rotation. This can be done with a callback:

```
void MouseWheel(GLFWwindow *w, double xoffset, double direction) {
    // registered with glfwSetScrollCallback
    // xoffset is amount of wheel rotation
    ...
```

6.7 Geometric Notes

Now that our application uses matrices and can rotate an object in three dimensions, it is useful to summarize elementary operations and notation for matrix algebra and vector geometry.

Rules for Matrix Multiplication

The product of two 4 X 4 matrices is a 4 X 4 matrix whose elements each represent the dot product of a row of the first matrix (corresponding to the row of the element being computed for the result) with a column of the second matrix (corresponding to the column of the resulting element). This is readily implemented (see VecMat.h).

The identity matrix I is a square matrix whose elements are all 0 except those along the diagonal, which are 1. Multiplication by I does not alter a matrix:

$MI = M$

The inverse of a M^{-1} of a matrix is such that: $MM^{-1} = I$.

The transpose M^T of a matrix swaps elements across the matrix diagonal, that is, M[i][j] is exchanged with M[j][i].

Based on the multiplication rules, the following identities can be deduced:

$A(B+C) = AB+AC$

$(A+B)^T = A^T+B^T$

$(AB)^T = B^TA^T$

$(A^{-1})^T = (A^T)^{-1}$

Additional matrix properties and operations are discussed in numerous texts.

A Summary of Vector Geometry

Length $|v| = (v \cdot v)^{1/2}$

Negation $-v = (-v_x, -v_y, -v_z)$

Scale $sv = (sv_x, sv_y, sv_z)$

Unitization $u = v\,/\,|v|$

Addition $v_1+v_2 = (v_{1x}+v_{2x},\ v_{1y}+v_{2y},\ v_{1z}+v_{2z})$

Dot Product (also called *scalar* or *inner* product)
The dot product of two 3D vectors yields a scalar
$$v_1 \bullet v_2 = v_{1x}v_{2x} + v_{1y}v_{2y} + v_{1z}v_{2z}$$
For unit-length v_1 and v_2, $v_1 \bullet v_2 = \cos\theta$, where θ is angle between vectors

Cross Product (also called vector or outer product)
The cross product of two 3D vectors yields a vector
$$v_1 \times v_2 = (v_{1y}v_{2z}-v_{1z}v_{2y},\ v_{1z}v_{2x}-v_{1x}v_{2z},\ v_{1x}v_{2y}-v_{1y}v_{2x})$$
This is a 'right-handed' cross-product: if right thumb is v_1, 1st finger is v_2, then 2nd finger points towards $v_1 \times v_2$; $v_1 \times v_2$: is perpendicular to v_1 and to v_2.

Point/Point Distance $|p_2 - p_1|$

Interpolation	$p_1 + t\,(p_2 - p1)$
Perpendicularity	$v_1 \bullet v_2 = 0$
Co-planarity 3 Vectors	$v_1 \bullet (v_2 \times v_3) = 0$
Parallelness 2 Vectors	$v_1 \bullet v_2 = \lvert v_1 \rvert\ \lvert v_2 \rvert$
Projection of v₁ onto v₂	$\left(\dfrac{v1 \bullet v2}{v2 \bullet v2} \right) v_2$

Staying Centered

To rotate a point about a fixed center (c_x, c_y), move to c origin, rotate, then move back:

$x' = c_x + (x-c_x)\cos\theta - (y-c_y)\sin\theta$
$y' = c_y + (x-c_x)\sin\theta + (y-c_y)\cos\theta$

These three steps can be represented in matrix form, but, although we write the steps above 'move c to origin', 'rotate', 'move back' from left to right, we code the corresponding matrices right to left, so that the first step is nearest **p**

$p' = T(c)R(\theta)T(-c)p$

In code:

```
vec3 pTransform = Translate(c)*RotateZ(θ)*Translate(-c)*vec4(p, 1);
```

Similarly, to scale a point p with respect to a fixed center (c_x, c_y), move p, scale, then move back:

$x' = c_x + s_x(p_x - c_x);$
$y' = c_y + s_y(p_y - c_y)$

In matrix form:

$p' = T(c)S(s)T(-c)p$

In code:

```
vec3 pTransform = Translate(c)*Scale(s)*Translate(-c)*vec4(p, 1);
```

Planes

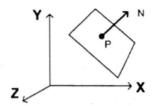

Figure 6-6: Plane geometry

The plane with normal n passing through a point p is given by $(a, b, c, d) = (n_x, n_y, n_z, -p{\cdot}n)$.

If (a, b, c) is unit-length, then the distance from a point (x, y, z) to the plane is given by $ax+by+cz+d$; the value is zero for a point on the plane.

Chapter 7: Perspective

7.1 Projective Transformations

The previous chapter described two groups of geometric transformations:

1) Euclidean transformations ('rigid body' operations that include rotation, translation, and, sometimes, reflection) are such that angles remain congruent, the distance between any two points is unchanged, parallelism is preserved, and straight lines remain straight.

2) Affine transformations (Euclidean transformations as well as uniform or differential scale and shear) are such that parallelism and ratio of parallel distances are preserved.

Projective transformations form a third group, in which points are projected along rays (*projectors*) that emanate from a *center of projection*. If the center of projection is infinitely far, then the rays are parallel and the transformation is a *parallel projection*; otherwise, the center is finite, the rays diverge, and the transformation is a *perspective projection*. With projective transformations, straight lines remain straight, but none of the other Euclidean or affine properties (congruency, distances, and parallelism) hold.

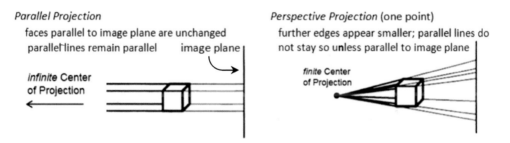

Figure 7-1: Parallel and perspective planar projections

If points in a scene are projected along rays to an *image plane*, the result is a *planar geometric projection*, i.e., a flat, two-dimensional image. OpenGL is optimized for this form of rendering.

Parallel projections are useful for design and manufacture, but they do not produce realistic images. As first understood during the Renaissance (see Fig. 3-1), realism requires perspective projection.

7.2 Perspective Transformations

Chapter 6 described the use of homogeneous coordinates to support translation and, in particular, allow a 4 X 4 matrix multiplication to represent any combination of scale, rotation, and translation. Of this Larry Roberts wrote in 1966, "The use of homogeneous coordinates throughout is extremely important in order to maintain the simplicity of the results, although its original purpose was to allow perspective transformations."

Both parallel and perspective planar projections may be represented by a 4 X 4 *projective transformation matrix.*

To understand the perspective transformation and its influence on our programming, we must examine the homogeneous coordinate point more closely. As Peter Shirley observed, "This 4D coordinate system is one of the most subtle and beautiful constructs used in computer science and it is certainly the biggest intellectual hurdle to jump when learning computer graphics."

7.3 Homogeneous Coordinates

Homogeneous coordinates allow perspective transformations because they inherently represent division: by definition, two homogeneous points, one a scalar multiple of the other, are equivalent. That is, the following two conversions hold:

1) An "ordinary" 3D point is converted to a 4D homogeneous point with the addition of a fourth coordinate, w, set to 1:

$$(x, y, z) \Rightarrow (x, y, z, 1)$$

2) A 4D homogeneous point is converted to an ordinary 3D point with the division by w of the first three coordinates:

$$(x, y, z, w) \Rightarrow (x/w, y/w, z/w)$$

The conversion from homogeneous to ordinary point implies that two homogeneous points, one a scalar multiple of the other, are equivalent; that is, $(x, y, z, w) \sim (kx, ky, kz, kw)$. It also implies that variation in w acts as a projection.

Projection to the w = 1 Plane

To illustrate (using a 2D, not 3D, example), consider an ordinary 2D point (x, y) and its 3D homogeneous equivalent $(x, y, 1)$, shown below in a three-dimensional homogeneous coordinate system.

The conversion from homogeneous point (x, y, w) to ordinary point $(x/w, y/w)$ is shown below as a line from the origin to the homogeneous point. The division by w acts as a projection, moving the point along the line to the $w = 1$ plane.

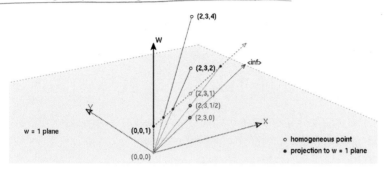

Figure 7-2: Division by the homogeneous coordinate

This is shown for five homogeneous points $(2, 3, w)$, with w of 4, 2, 1, ½, and 0. Their projections to the $w = 1$ plane are shown as a series of solid blue (and one red) dots.

Points at Infinity

As w approaches 0 in the above illustration, the projection moves along the dashed red line and, in the limit, reaches a *point at infinity* in the (2, 3) direction. A point at infinity is equivalent to a direction, i.e., a vector. That is, a 3D homogeneous point $(x, y, 0)$ is equivalent to an ordinary 2D vector (x, y), whereas a 3D homogeneous point $(x, y, 1)$ is equivalent to an ordinary 2D point (x, y).

When a 4D homogeneous point at infinity is multiplied by a 4 X 4 affine transformation matrix A (whose 4th row is (0, 0, 0, 1)), the resulting w is 0:

$$A \begin{bmatrix} x \\ y \\ z \\ 0 \end{bmatrix} = \begin{bmatrix} x' \\ y' \\ z' \\ w' \end{bmatrix} = \begin{bmatrix} x' \\ y' \\ z' \\ 0 \end{bmatrix}$$

That is, the result remains a point at infinity. In effect, the translation components of the affine transformation are ignored.

7.4 The Perspective Matrix

Within the 4 X 4 affine transformation matrix, different elements control different aspects of the transformation. In the representation below, the **s** elements refer to scale, **r** refers to rotation, and **t** refers to translation. The product of the affine matrix with any homogeneous point (x, y, z, 1) results in w′ = 1.

$$
\begin{bmatrix} s & r & r & t \\ r & s & r & t \\ r & r & s & t \\ 0 & 0 & 0 & 1 \end{bmatrix}
\begin{bmatrix} x \\ y \\ z \\ 1 \end{bmatrix}
=
\begin{bmatrix} x' \\ y' \\ z' \\ w' \end{bmatrix}
=
\begin{bmatrix} x' \\ y' \\ z' \\ 1 \end{bmatrix}
$$

In contrast, the following *projection* matrix, which has a non-zero element, 1/D (in the 'w' row and 'z' column), results in w′ being proportional to z.

$$
\begin{bmatrix} 1 & 0 & 0 & 0 \\ 0 & 1 & 0 & 0 \\ 0 & 0 & 1 & 0 \\ 0 & 0 & 1/D & 0 \end{bmatrix}
\begin{bmatrix} x \\ y \\ z \\ 1 \end{bmatrix}
=
\begin{bmatrix} x' \\ y' \\ z' \\ w' \end{bmatrix}
=
\begin{bmatrix} x \\ y \\ z \\ z/D \end{bmatrix}
\sim (xD/z,\ yD/z,\ D)
$$

To compute the equivalent ordinary point thus requires a division by z. This division is called the *perspective divide*. The effect on z is a projection to the z′ = D plane, but the effect on x and y is a scale that produces similar triangles, shown below in the YZ plane.

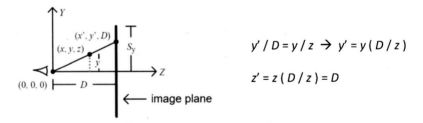

$$ y'/D = y/z \rightarrow y' = y(D/z) $$

$$ z' = z(D/z) = D $$

Figure 7-3: Projection to the image plane (viewed edge on)

The division by z is a non-linear operation in three dimensions, but it is formulated as a linear relationship in four dimensions (i.e., matrix multiplication of a homogeneous point is a linear operation, but the perspective divide is not).

59

If a vector (i.e., point-at-infinity) is multiplied by a perspective transformation matrix (or the combination of an affine and perspective matrix), the result has a non-zero homogeneous coordinate (unlike the case with an affine transformation); the homogeneous divide and projection to the image plane yields the *vanishing point* for the vector. For example, given a pair of railroad tracks, one need only know their direction to determine the point on a perspective image where they disappear.

Maintaining a Range for z'

With the previous matrix, all points are projected onto the $z = D$ plane. This loss of depth information is due to the linear dependence of the third and fourth rows of the matrix. The linear dependence also means the matrix is non-invertible.

It is preferable that z' vary for several reasons: the matrix will be invertible, and z' can be used for clipping and depth comparison (described in the next section).

In the perspective matrix below, the non-zero term in the fourth column does not affect x' and y', but z' becomes $D-D/z$. For $z = 1$, $z' = 0$, and for $z = \infty$, $z' = D$. Thus, the Euclidean space $z \in (1, \infty)$ is compressed to $z' \in (0, D)$.

$$\begin{bmatrix} 1 & 0 & 0 & 0 \\ 0 & 1 & 0 & 0 \\ 0 & 0 & 1 & -1 \\ 0 & 0 & 1/D & 0 \end{bmatrix} \begin{bmatrix} x \\ y \\ z \\ 1 \end{bmatrix} = \begin{bmatrix} x \\ y \\ z-1 \\ z/D \end{bmatrix} \sim \left(\frac{Dx}{z}, \frac{Dy}{z}, D(z-1)/z \right) = \left(\frac{Dx}{z}, \frac{Dy}{z}, D-D/z \right)$$

The View Frustum

Conventional displays are flat and rectangular, so the projectors of a perspective image sweep out a pyramidal volume, with the eye at the apex and bounded by left, right, bottom and top planes. When also bounded by near and far planes, the resulting truncated pyramid is called a *view frustum*.

The view frustum is in *eye space* (also called *camera space*); that is, ordinary space with the x-axis to the right, the y-axis up, and the eye at the origin looking down the negative z-axis. Although the above example produces $z' \in (0, D)$, OpenGL expects perspective matrices to yield a canonical space of +/-1 in x' and y', and $z' \in (0, 1)$. And so, the elements of a perspective matrix are scaled accordingly, as can be seen in VecMat.h.

Thus, for example, the left plane in eye space is transformed to the $x = -1$ plane in perspective space.

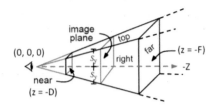

Figure 7-4: Eye space

After the perspective transformation and perspective divide, the view frustum above becomes a rectilinear solid, below. The top and bottom planes have become parallel, as have the left/right and near/far.

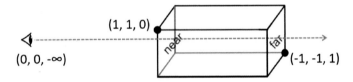

Figure 7-5: Perspective space

Points in *perspective space* are given in *normalized device coordinates*. The location of a point on the screen is determined solely by a point's x and y coordinates in this space.

Another illustration is given below in terms of the effect of the perspective transformation on geometry. At left, in eye space, a row of equal-sized numerals aligns with the z-axis; the eye is at the middle of the '5' looking towards the '9'; the near and far planes bracket the '7'. The frustum is cross-hatched.

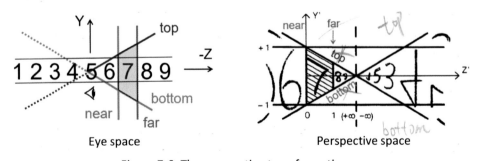

Figure 7-6: The perspective transformation

In perspective space, after the perspective divide, the eye is infinitely far to the left (towards +z'), and so the nearest object the eye sees is the oversized front of the '5'. It then sees '6' through '9', which decrease in size. The infinitely distant become zero in size, +inf wraps to −inf, and the space behind the eye is transformed so that it sees an inverted '1' proceeding to the rear half of an inverted '5'.

In the next section we discuss clipping, which limits the display to the view frustum.

7.5 Additional Stages in the Graphics Pipeline

There are additional stages in the graphics pipeline that were omitted in chapter 1 but are now relevant. These include three stages before the rasterizer: *primitive assembly*, *clipping against the view frustum*, and the *viewport transformation*. Following the rasterizer is a *depth-test*. These stages are handled automatically by OpenGL, but they influence the design of the perspective matrix and the vertex shader.

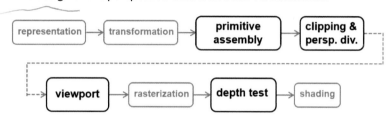

Figure 7-7: Additional stages in the graphics pipeline

Primitive Assembly

The pipeline receives a sequence of vertices from GPU memory. Every n vertices is treated as a *primitive*, i.e., a point ($n = 1$), segment ($n = 2$), triangle ($n = 3$), or quadrilateral ($n = 4$). The fetch of vertices commences with a call to *glDrawArrays* or *glDrawElements*; n is implied by the first argument (GL_POINTS, GL_LINES, GL_TRIANGLES, or GL_QUADS). The 'assembly' of the primitive is simply a grouping of its vertices.

Clipping and the Perspective Divide

Once a primitive is assembled, it is clipped against the view frustum. Clipping against the left, right, top and bottom planes prevents unneeded rasterization. In the example below, a portion of a large triangle, shown as dashed, is clipped and the remaining part is converted to two smaller triangles, that are then rasterized.

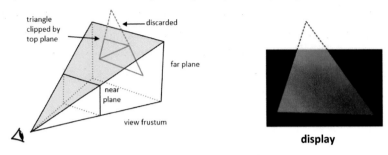

Figure 7-8: Clipping to the view frustum

Consider the need to clip against a near plane: referring to the perspective matrix, w' is proportional to z, which is to say that if z is negative, then z' and w' are negative, and z'/w' is positive. That is (see Fig. 7-6), points behind the eye transform to the front of the eye unless clipped before the perspective division. For this reason, the vertex shader sets the homogeneous transformed point $gl\_Position$ without performing the division.

Although clipping could be performed in eye space, it is simpler to perform in perspective space (that is, after the perspective transformation but before the perspective divide). For example, the right clipping plane after the divide must be at $x = 1$, which means clipping in homogeneous space is (trivially) against the $x = w$ plane.

The projection transformations presume a camera at the origin, facing the negative z-axis. The near clipping plane should be a distance N along the negative z-axis, and the far clipping plane a greater distance F along the negative z-axis, with $F > N > 0$ ($N = .005$ and $F = 1000$ are reasonable defaults).

OpenGL automatically performs clipping and then the perspective divide. Upon completion,

> $gl\_Position.xy/gl\_Position.w$ is in a *normalized device space* of +/-1
> $gl\_Position.z/gl\_Position.w$ is used by the rasterizer for the depth test.

Viewport Transformation

After clipping and the perspective divide, a vertex is in *perspective space*, canonically defined as +/-1 in x and y and 0-1 in z. The +/-1 xy range is mapped to pixel coordinates by the *viewport transformation*, a simple two-dimensional scale and translation to *screen space*. In this space the rasterizer determines those pixels that are to be shaded.

Screen space dimensions are the same as the application's window; on initialization, the OpenGL viewport defaults to the full window. If, however, there are multiple viewports (i.e., sub-windows), the mouse down callback must determine which viewport contains the mouse, and call *glViewport* accordingly. This is because some interactive operations (see chapter 11) require a pixel location given a 3D point, or a 3D line given a pixel; in both cases, the current viewport is used.

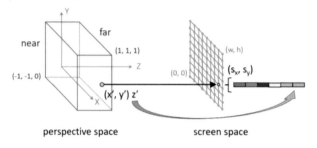

Figure 7-9: The viewport transformation

The viewport transformation is relevant whenever a user resizes the application window. Consider our example from chapter 4, which requests an application window sized 600 by 600:

```
GLFWwindow *w = glfwCreateWindow(600, 600, "Colorful Triangle", NULL, NULL);
```

This means the entire viewport is mapped to the 600 by 600 pixel window. If the window is later resized, the viewport is unchanged; it still maps to a 600 by 600 window. This results in the image being clipped if one of the dimensions is shortened, or being stretched if one of the dimensions is lengthened.

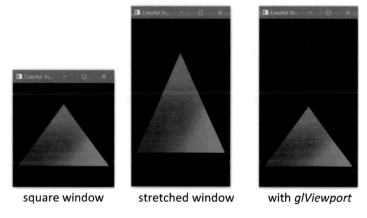

square window   stretched window   with *glViewport*

Figure 7-10: Resizing a window

64

This is because a default OpenGL viewport is set to the window when it is created, i.e., origin at (0,0) and size (width, height).

A means to prevent the distortion is

```
int width, height;
glfwGetWindowSize(w, &width, &height);
int minSize = width < height? width : height;
glViewport(0, 0, minSize, minSize);
```

But this solution confines the rendering to only part of the window.

To avoid distortion when rendering to a non-square window, the view transformation must compensate. This is done in the Orthographic and Perspective subroutines in VecMat.h. Both routines adjust the relative scale between the X and Y axes according to the aspect ratio of the application window (or sub-window).

So that the program can respond should a user resize the window, a callback procedure can be provided:

```
void Resize(GLFWwindow *w, int width, int height) {
    // recompute perspective matrix and reset viewport
    persp = Perspective(fieldOfView, aspectRatio, nearDst, farDst);
    glViewport(0, 0, width, height);
}
```

It can be registered in *main* with *glfwSetWindowSizeCallback*.

Depth Test

The perspective space *z* value (in the range 0 to 1) is also stored in the pixel (see figure 7-9), so that a typical pixel consists of one byte each for red, green, blue, and alpha, and two bytes for depth. This depth layer of the pixel is the *depth buffer* (or *z-buffer*).

After the viewport transformation, but before the pixel shader, a *depth-test* is executed to prevent the call to the pixel shader if the pixel has already been shaded and has a closer *z*-value. The rasterizer automatically interpolates *gl_Position.z* for use in the test.

The depth test solves the *hidden surface problem*; it prevents an object that is behind something from obscuring it, regardless of the order of rendering. It is a general method used since the 1970s. There are times, however, when we will disable the depth test.

As mentioned, the distance to the near and far clipping planes can be given reasonable defaults. But if the scene extends a known distance, it is prudent to set *N* and *F* accordingly; the smaller their difference, the higher is the precision of *z*-buffer entries.

7.6 Exercise: CubePersp.cpp

In the solution to the exercise in chapter 6, we interactively rotated a 2D letter in three dimensions. For this exercise, we wish to add:

  1) a perspective view,
  2) interactive adjustment of the field of view, and
  3) display of an object with volume, both shaded and line-drawn

The Cube

Rather than a flat letter, it is easier to demonstrate perspective with a solid object. A cube is a good choice as its parallel and equal-length edges show changes in length and parallelism on the image plane (i.e., the display).

We can define a colorful cube as eight points centered about the origin, connected into six square faces:

```
float l = -1, r = 1, b = -1, t = 1, n = -1, f = 1;  // left, right, bottom, top, near, far
float points[][3] = {{l,b,n}, {l,b,f}, {l,t,n}, {l,t,f}, {r,b,n}, {r,b,f}, {r,t,n}, {r,t,f}};    // 8 points
float colors[][3] = {{0,0,1}, {0,1,0}, {0,1,1}, {1,0,0}, {1,0,1}, {1,1,0}, {0,0,0}, {1,1,1}}; // 8 colors
int faces[][4] = {{1,3,2,0}, {6,7,5,4}, {4,5,1,0}, {3,7,6,2}, {2,6,4,0}, {5,7,3,1}};    // 6 faces
```

The field of view, and scale and stretch factors for the cube should be defined:

```
float fieldOfView = 30, cubeSize = .05f, cubeStretch = cubeSize;
```

The stretch factor will allow us to expand the cube along the *z*-axis, to emphasize the foreshortening due to perspective.

Changes to shaders

To accommodate the 3D points, the vertex shader input "point" should be declared a vec3, not vec2. The assignment to *gl_Position* must change accordingly:

```
gl_Position = view*vec4(point, 1);
```

No change is needed to the pixel shader, but several are needed to *Display*.

Movement along the z-axis

It is useful to modify the default value for tranNew because the cube is defined about the origin; moving it away from the eye avoids the near clipping plane.

```
vec3 tranOld, tranNew(0,0,-1);              // old/new translate
```

Concerning clipping, we'll change the MouseWheel function from the last exercise so that it controls dolly; this allows us to experiment with the effects of the near clipping plane. So rather than modify *rotZ*, we modify *tranNew*:

```
tranNew.z += direction > 0? -.1f : .1f;     // dolly in/out
```

Depth Test

The cube is the first object we've rendered that can obscure itself; thus, we enable the use of the *z*-buffer. At the beginning of *Display*, add:

```
glClear(GL_DEPTH_BUFFER_BIT);
glEnable(GL_DEPTH_TEST);
```

The depth test works for points, lines, triangles and quads.

Other Changes to Display

As the vertex data is now 3D, establishing the vertex feed must change to:

```
VertexAttribPointer(program, "point", 3, 0, (void *) 0);
```

If we change *Display* to accept a *GLFWwindow *w* argument, we can obtain the current display size (in pixels) with the following:

```
int screenWidth, screenHeight;
glfwGetWindowSize(w, &screenWidth, &screenHeight);
```

This enables us to compare a solid rendering with a line drawing by dividing the screen into left and right viewports. So, the aspect ratio is computed by:

```
int halfWidth = screenWidth/2
float aspectRatio = (float) halfWidth / (float) screenHeight;
```

The *Perspective* subroutine in VecMat.h accepts near and far clipping plane distances and derives the left, right, top and bottom planes from the field of view and aspect ratio. It then constructs a matrix similar to that of sec 7.4.

```
float nearDistance = .001f, farDistance = 500;          // + distance along -z axis
mat4 persp = Perspective(fieldOfView, aspectRatio, nearDistance, farDistance);
```

A *modelview* matrix is computed as the product of several affine transformations. `tranNew` is now a vec3, so it can be passed as a single argument to *Translate*:

```
mat4 scale = Scale(cubeSize, cubeSize, cubeStretch);  // unit cube too big, z stretch
mat4 rot = RotateY(rotNew.x)*RotateX(rotNew.y);       // mouse-specified
mat4 tran = Translate(tranNew);                        // mouse-specified
mat4 modelview = tran*rot*scale;                       // all affine transformations
mat4 view = persp*modelview;                           // one matrix for all xforms
SetUniform(program, "view", view);                     // send to shader
```

To shade the cube on the left of the display, we set the viewport to the left half of the screen. And we replace GL_TRIANGLES with GL_QUADS; the number of vertices to fetch is the number of elements in the faces array.

```
glViewport(0, 0, halfWidth, screenHeight);            // left half of app: solid cube
glDrawElements(GL_QUADS, sizeof(faces)/sizeof(int), GL_UNSIGNED_INT, faces);
```

On the right half of the display, we'll create a lined version, one cube face at a time using *glDrawElements*. GL_LINE_LOOP, rather than GL_QUADS, causes OpenGL to draw lines between sequential vertices and to connect the last to the first.

```
glViewport(halfWidth, 0, halfWidth, screenHeight);    // right half: line-drawn cube
glLineWidth(5);
for (int i = 0; i < 6; i++)                            // draw outline each face
    glDrawElements(GL_LINE_LOOP, 4, GL_UNSIGNED_INT, &faces[i]);
```

The display should look like:

Figure 7-11: Cube shaded and drawn in perspective

68

Bonus: interactive field of view and cube stretch

We can interactively adjust the field of view and the cube stretch factor with the keyboard. We use a callback to respond to key presses of *f* (increase field of view) or *s* (increase stretch); holding the SHIFT key causes a decrease:

```
void Key(GLFWwindow *w, int key, int scancode, int action, int mods) {
    bool shift = mods & GLFW_MOD_SHIFT;
    if (action == GLFW_PRESS)
        switch (key) {
            case GLFW_KEY_ESCAPE:
                glfwSetWindowShouldClose(w, GLFW_TRUE);
                break;
            case 'F':
                fieldOfView += shift? -5 : 5;
                fieldOfView = fieldOfView < 5? 5 : fieldOfView > 150? 150 : fieldOfView;
                break;
            case 'S':
                cubeStretch *= shift? .9f : 1.1f;
                cubeStretch = cubeStretch < .02f? .02f : cubeStretch;
                break;
        }
}
```

Adjusting the stretch yields images with obvious foreshortening:

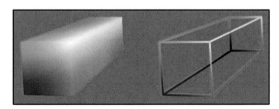

Figure 7-12: Stretched cube in perspective

69

Chapter 8: Camera and Scene

The transformations we have developed in the previous chapters are central to the placement of objects within a scene, and the creation of an image of a scene. To understand this use, we need to consider a few "spaces" and how transformations take us from one space to another.

8.1 Coordinate Systems

In chapter 9 we will see that it is in *eye space* that we must evaluate the illumination of a scene, but it is in *perspective space* that rasterization and bilinear interpolation of vertex attributes occur. This implies (for shaded images) that the vertex shader must transform input points into two different spaces, which is why the *modelview* and *perspective* transformations are typically sent separately to the vertex shader.

We review the vertex shader in detail at the end of this chapter.

Object Space and World Space

An individual object is modeled in *object* (sometimes called *model*) *space*; an associated geometry matrix *G* transforms it to *world* (sometimes called *scene*) space.

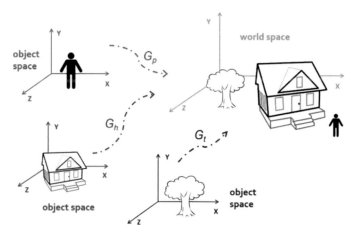

Figure 8-1: Object spaces and world space

Eye Space

The eye transformation E is a matrix that transforms world space to *eye* (or *camera*) space. This is a space defined such that the eye (camera) is at the origin, looking down the negative z-axis, with the y-axis defining upwards.

A point defined in object space can be transformed to eye space via multiple transformations.

$$p' = EGp$$

where G is a transformation of point p into world space and E is a transformation from world space into eye space.

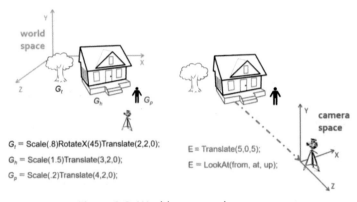

$G_t = \text{Scale}(.8)\text{RotateX}(45)\text{Translate}(2,2,0);$
$G_h = \text{Scale}(1.5)\text{Translate}(3,2,0);$
$G_p = \text{Scale}(.2)\text{Translate}(4,2,0);$

$E = \text{Translate}(5,0,5);$
$E = \text{LookAt}(\text{from, at, up});$

Figure 8-2: World space and eye space

The G (geometry) and E (camera) matrices may be concatenated into a single view matrix, $M = E\,G$, as, for example, in the exercise in chapter 7. A matrix must be computed for each object (using its corresponding G_i) in the scene.

Matrix multiplications are written symbolically left to right, but their effect on $(x, y, z, 1)$ is accumulated from right to left. That is, the point (x, y, z) goes from object, to world, to eye space. In terms of the present implementation, *multiplication of matrices coded left to right is the reverse order of the transformations as applied to a point*. That is, the point is written last and the matrix closest to the point is the first transformation applied to the point. This is summarized in the following illustration.

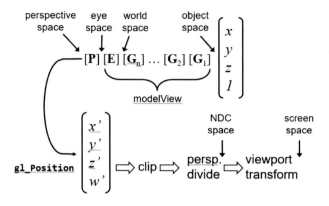

Figure 8-3: modelView and perspective matrices

$G_1 \dots G_n$ are affine transforms (scale, move, or rotate). Each object has an individual set of these transformations; after their application, the objects reside in a common, world (or scene) space.

E is the world space to eye space transform; after this transformation the camera is considered to be at the origin, facing down the negative z-axis. This matrix may be specified as a series of transformations, or as a single transformation derived from the camera and look-at locations and the up direction (see *LookAt* in VecMat.h).

If an object is to be illuminated by a light and shaded accordingly, the calculations will be performed in eye space.

P is a perspective transformation. A point (x', y', z', w') transformed through P is in perspective space; the primitive is then ready to be clipped. After the perspective divide and viewport transform, the primitive is ready to be rasterized.

Where is the Camera?

In the case where the camera location is specified interactively as a series of rotations and translations, the final location in world space can be found by transforming the camera in eye space, which by definition is at the origin, by the inverse transform of the [E] matrix.

For example, consider the unit cube we defined in chapter 7; it is centered at the origin. By default, the camera is located at the origin, and therefore most of the cube is not visible. We applied a translation of (0, 0, -10) to the modelview matrix, so that the cube locations were translated -10 in Z. This transformation will be applied to all vertices coming into the vertex shader. In this case, the camera is now 10 units away from the cube, rather than being at its center.

If we ask the question where is the camera in the original world space, the answer is necessarily that the camera is at (0, 0, 10). This is the inverse question of where does the origin transform to in eye space. So, the modelview transformation applied to the cube has the inverse effect on the camera.

Thus, given the modelview matrix M, the location of the camera in world space is given by:

$$\begin{bmatrix} cx \\ cy \\ cz \\ 1 \end{bmatrix} = M^{-1} \begin{bmatrix} 0 \\ 0 \\ 0 \\ 1 \end{bmatrix}$$

8.2 A Camera Class

In our recent examples and exercises, we've relied upon the mouse (and keyboard) to move or rotate the camera. Although the application must still register handlers for mouse events, much of the camera computation and state can be stored in a class, resulting in a better organized application.

The class defined in Camera.h manages the rotation and translation parameters needed for mouse down and mouse drag, and provides access to the modelview and perspective matrices.

The class also provides the subroutine *SetRotateCenter*; when passed a 3D point, all future rotations will occur about it as center. This is a valuable capability, especially when attempting to look closely at something, from different angles.

[There is a subtlety concerning this operation: when changing the center of rotation, the angles of rotation do not themselves change. When those same rotations are applied using a different center of rotation, however, the orientation of the object will not change, but its position within the scene will. It is important to accommodate this change in the center of rotation with a translation offset. Initially the offset is zero, but for each change in the center of rotation, it is recomputed.]

73

8.3 Review of Vertex Shader Code

The need for lighting calculations requires separate *persp* and *modelview* matrices, so that points and surface normals may be transformed by the modelview matrix only. These are explicitly declared as outputs *vPoint* and *vNormal*.

The purely graphical operations implemented by OpenGL (primitive formation, clipping, perspective division, rasterization, and depth comparison) require only the built-in variable *gl_Position*, which is the input point transformed by the modelview and perspective matrices into 4D homogeneous perspective space.

This explains the input and output arrangement for the following, typical vertex shader (except in chapter 12 we'll learn that rather than *vec3 color*, *vec2 textureCoordinates* is typically given as an input).

```
1  char *vertexShader = "\
2       #version 130
3       in vec3 point;
4       in vec3 normal;
5       in vec3 color;
6       out vec3 vPoint;
7       out vec3 vNormal;
8       out vec3 vColor;
9       uniform mat4 modelview;
10      uniform mat4 persp;
11      void main() {
12          vPoint = (modelview*vec4(point, 1).xyz;
13          vNormal = (modelview*vec4(normal, 0)).xyz;
14          gl_Position = persp*vec4(vPoint, 1);
15          vColor = color;
16      }";
```

Lines 3-5: The vertex feeder is expected to send three vertex attributes: point (location), surface normal at the point, and color. These attributes are stored in the GPU vertex buffer.

Lines 6-8: These are the named outputs of the vertex shader; *point* and *normal* were input from object space, but the output *vPoint* and *vNormal* are in eye space; the built-in output *gl_Position* is in perspective space.

Lines 9-10: The application's *Display* computes the *modelview* and *persp* matrices and passes them as uniforms to the vertex shader. *modelview* is the combination of transformations that bring the vertices from object space to camera space, *e.g.*, *GE*. If there is to be no shading, then a single matrix can be used:

```
mat4 view = persp*modelview;
```

Line 12: The shader computes the product of *modelview* and *point* (promoted to a vec4 homogeneous point, i.e., *w* = 1). Because *modelview* is an affine transformation, the product yields *w* = 1, which is to say that the result, *vPoint*, is an ordinary point in camera space. Once the primitive is assembled and clipped, the rasterizer will, on a pixel by pixel basis, interpolate *vPoint* and send it to the pixel shader, where it is used for lighting calculations.

Line 13: The shader computes the product of *modelview* and *normal* (promoted to a vec4 homogeneous *vector*, i.e., *w* = 0); the result, just as with *vPoint*, exists in camera space. The rasterizer will interpolate *vNormal* and send it to the pixel shader for lighting calculations.

Line 14: The shader computes the product of *vPoint*, which exists in camera space, with *persp*. The result, defined in homogeneous perspective space, is assigned to gl_*Position*, a built-in output variable.

Line 15: The input *color* is assigned, unchanged, to *vColor*, which will be interpolated by the rasterizer and sent to the pixel shader.

The perspective divide (division by gl_*Position.w*) is not performed by the vertex shader. It is automatically performed by OpenGL after a primitive has been clipped by the view frustum (clipping prevents points behind the eye being inverted forward by the division). The division yields a point in perspective space that is then transformed by the viewport. The rasterizer interpolates these points to determine those pixels to be sent to the pixel shader.

8.4 Exercise

Revise the previous exercise (CubePersp) to use the Camera class. The camera should be declared at the top of the file:

```
int winWidth = 500, winHeight = 500;
Camera camera(winWidth/2, winHeight, vec3(0,0,0), vec3(0,0,-1), 30);
```

This declares a camera with no initial rotation, but an initial translation by -1 in *Z*, and a field of view of 30 degrees. The camera width is set to half the screen's width, as we display one half of screen at a time (as in CubePersp).

There is no scale capability within the camera, but a view matrix that incorporates scale can be created by:

```
mat4 m = camera.fullview*Scale(cubeSize, cubeSize, cubeStretch);
SetUniform(program, "view", m);
```

Finally, in all the mouse callbacks, replace internal code with the appropriate call to Camera.h. For example, in MouseButton, rather than modify the variables *mouseDown*, *rotOld*, and *tranOld*, simply call camera.MouseDown or camera.MouseUp.

Chapter 9: Shading

In 1968, Ivan Sutherland and David Evans established a federally funded program of computer graphics research at the University of Utah; PhD graduates include John Warnock (Adobe), Jim Clark (Silicon Graphics), and Ed Catmull (Pixar). Evans and Sutherland also founded their namesake company to commercialize a new industry as well as to build hardware to support the university research.

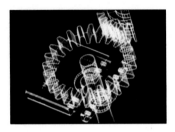 

Figure 9-1: The Picture System was a line drawing (vector) device for 3D scenes, useful for design and night flight simulation. Sutherland and Evans examine circuitry, 1969. (courtesy Evans & Sutherland Computer Corp.)

The early devices were *line drawing*. Greater realism required *shaded images* created by applying a model of surface illumination at individual pixels of a raster.

9.1 Lighting

To assign an *rgb* value to a pixel, an *illumination model* calculates the brightness of the surface at the pixel. For an *ideal diffuse* surface, the amount of light reflected, according to Lambert, depends on the incoming light direction L and the surface normal N.

For a perfect diffuser, reflected light is omnidirectional, i.e, the angle between N and the eye direction does not affect the intensity. If L and N are unit length, the cosine of the angle between them equals their dot product (provable with the *Law of Cosines*).

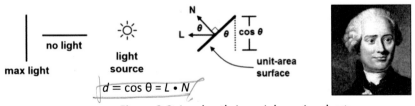

Figure 9-2: Lambert's Law; Johann Lambert

The vector L can be fixed as the direction towards an *infinite light* (such as the sun), or, if a light is *local*, the vector L will vary according to the surface location.

The diffuse intensity *d* is usually augmented with *ambient* and *specular* components; ambient light suffuses an area indirectly and can be mimicked as a small constant, *a*. Exponentiating the diffuse term produces a small bright region suggestive of a highlight. That is, a specular term was computed: $s = d^k$. Thus, an early shading formula was:

(9-1) $\quad I = max(0, min(1, a+d+s))$

$$ s = d^k $$

where *I* is intensity, *a* is the ambient term (perhaps ~ .15), *d* is the diffuse term, and *s* is the specular term, where *k* is large (> 50). Increasing *k* has the effect of 'sharpening' the cosine, producing a smaller, brighter region.

Equation (9-1) assumes the eye is on the same side of the surface as the light and the surface normal faces the light. This is "one-sided" shading, which is appropriate for closed, opaque objects. Two-sided shading, in which $d = |\cos \Theta| = abs(L \bullet N)$, is appropriate for an 'open' object (like a bowl) or a semi-transparent object.

Sutherland applied this formula to a Volkswagen Beetle digitized by graduate students in 1972. This produced the first object-recognizable computer-generated shaded image. Surface normals were calculated for each *facet* (quadrilateral or triangle).

Figure 9-3: Digitizing and rendering the VW Beetle
(in photograph, Ivan Sutherland is at left, Bui Tuong Phong is at right)

At that time, facets of an object were rendered sequentially, and it was straightforward to modulate the intensity on a facet-by-facet basis, yielding the above shaded image.

A similar approach is taken by *Display* in CubePersp.cpp, where faces are displayed sequentially to produce a line drawing. This could be modified so that, for each face,

Display would calculate a surface normal, apply (9-1), and send the resulting intensity to the vertex shader via a uniform variable. The uniform would then modulate the output:

```
uniform float intensity;
...
vColor = vec4(intensity*color, 1);
```

This approach is poor for large numbers of faces because a) update of shader uniforms is relatively slow, and b) the CPU processes the faces sequentially, whereas the GPU can process them in parallel. It is more efficient for the face normals to reside in GPU memory and the vertex shader to perform the shading calculation. This is implemented in the next section.

9.2 Faceted Shading

With faceted shading, the surface normal of the primitive (i.e., triangle or quadrilateral), not the vertex, is used for shading. But OpenGL shader architecture is driven by vertex buffers. Thus, for a given vertex, coincident (same position) vertices must be created, one for each primitive that surrounds the vertex. Each of the coincident vertices has the same position, but a different surface normal.

We now consider the faceted rendering of a faceted object. Many objects, like the cube, are intentionally faceted; for some design tasks faceted shading is preferred. In this section, we describe the changes needed to 8-Solution-CubePerspCamera to convert the right side of the display from a line drawing to a faceted rendering, as below.

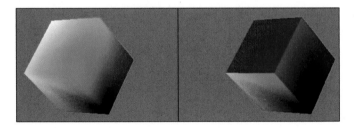

Figure 9-4: Original colorful cube (left) and faceted version

The pixel shader needs no modification. But to implement equation (9-1), the vertex shader needs, in addition to location and color, a surface normal:

    in vec3 normal;   // stored in vertex buffer

It also requires the light source direction (which is given a default):

    uniform vec3 lightVec = vec3(1,.5,-1);

In our last exercise, CubePersp.cpp, we sent a single matrix to the vertex shader. It represented the combination of geometric transformations and the perspective transformation. Its only use was to compute the homogeneous output *gl_Position*.

For faceted shading, however, we must send the matrices separately:

SetUniform(program, "modelview", modelview);
SetUniform(program, "persp", persp);

This allows the surface normal to be modified by *modelview*, but not by *persp*. Rather than a single "view" matrix, the vertex shader instead accepts two matrix uniforms:

    uniform mat4 modelview;
    uniform mat4 persp;

The body of the vertex shader is different, transforming a surface normal and applying (9-1):

```
// set gl_Position to input point transformed by both matrices:
gl_Position = persp*modelview*vec4(point, 1);
// transform normal by modelview, set to unit length:
vec3 xnormal = normalize((modelview*vec4(normal, 0)).xyz);
// ensure light vector is unit length:
vec3 vlight = normalize(lightVec);
// set ambient, two-sided diffuse, and specular coefficients:
float a = .1;
float d = abs(dot(xnormal, vlight));
float s = pow(d, 50);
// set intensity and output color:
float intensity = clamp(a+d+s, 0, 1);
vColor = intensity*color;
```

The input normal is promoted to a homogeneous point by adding a homogeneous coordinate of 0. The product with the matrix is a homogeneous point with $w = 0$. The

80

.xyz component of the result is the transformed vector. If the *modelview* transform contains any scale, however, the vector must be re-normalized.

Differential Scale and the Normal

Consider a 2D line through the origin and a point $p = (a, b)$. The direction of the line is $v_1 = (a, b)$. A second line, through the origin and perpendicular to the first, must necessarily be described by a direction vector $v_2 = (-b, a)$, or a scalar multiple thereof, because the dot product, $v_1 \cdot v_2$, must be zero.

If we scale (a, b) differentially, say by $(1, 2)$, p becomes $p' = (a, 2b)$. In order for v_2' to be perpendicular to v_1', it must equal $(-2b, a)$; so, whereas v_1' is v_1 stretched vertically, v_2' is v_2 stretched horizontally. That is, if a transformation with differential scale is applied to vertex locations, it cannot be applied to surface normals.

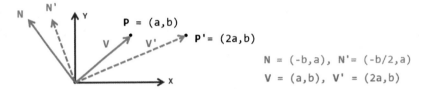

Figure 9-5: Stretching a point causes contraction of a normal

In the figure above, $N \cdot V = 0$. We can introduce a 2 X 2 matrix M, capable of rotation and uniform or differential scaling, and its inverse:

$$N \cdot M^{-1}MV = 0$$

because $M^{-1}MV = V$. If we move one matrix to the other side of the dot product (because both dot product and matrix multiplication are linear operations), and replace MV with the transformed V'

$NM^{-1} \cdot V' = 0$, suggesting NM^{-1} must equal N', or

$N' = M^{-1T}N$

That is, points transformed by M mean normals are transformed by M^{-1T} (the "inverse transpose").

This generalizes to three dimensions and 4 X 4 matrices. Transformations applied to vertex locations affect vertex normals inversely. In the case of a pure rotation, the

81

inverse-transpose is the same as the original; in the case of uniform scale, the inverse-transpose is a multiple of the original; thus, for uniform scale and/or pure rotations, the normal can be transformed (and then unitized) by the *modelview* matrix.

But if the scale is differential, the inverse-transpose must be used to transform the normal. If *M* is not invertible, the *matrix of co-factors* may be used to transform normals.

Duplication of Vertices

Modern graphics architecture is optimized to operate on GPU vertices; faces (triangles and quadrilaterals) are 'assembled' from them. If a face normal is to reside in GPU memory, it must be as a vertex attribute. As mentioned in the beginning of section 9.2, for faceted shading a separate vertex must be buffered for each face sharing the vertex.

For the cube, each corner is shared by three faces; thus, each corner appears as three separate vertices, all with the same location and color but each with a different surface normal. Rather than 8 vertices, 24 are stored.

Because a vertex now includes surface normal as well as location and color information, it is convenient to define (as we did in exercise 4.5) a vertex structure.

```
struct Vertex {
    vec3 point, color, normal;
    Vertex() { }
    Vertex(vec3 p, vec3 c, vec3 n) : point(p), color(c), normal(n) { }
};
Vertex vertices[24];
```

InitVertexBuffer must be modified to fill the vertex array from the given points, colors, and faces arrays, and then copy the vertex array to a GPU vertex buffer.

The vertex array is filled face by face; for each face, the surface normal is computed and then repeated for each of the four face vertices. Once filled, the vertex array is copied to the GPU with a single call:

```
// create vertex array
int nvrts = sizeof(faces)/sizeof(int), nfaces = nvrts/4;
int vsize = sizeof(Vertex);
for (int i = 0; i < nfaces; i++) {
```

```
  int *f = faces[i];
  vec3 p1(points[f[0]]), p2(points[f[1]]), p3(points[f[2]]);
  vec3 n = Normalize(Cross(p3-p2, p2-p1)); // use n for 4 face verts
  for (int k = 0; k < 4; k++) {
    int vid = f[k];
    vertices[4*i+k] = Vertex(vec3(points[vid]), vec3(colors[vid]), n);
  }
}
// create and bind GPU vertex buffer, copy vertex data
glGenBuffers(1, &vBuffer);
glBindBuffer(GL_ARRAY_BUFFER, vBuffer);
glBufferData(GL_ARRAY_BUFFER, nvrts*vsize, &vertices[0], GL_STATIC_DRAW);
```

There are several modifications needed to the application's *Display*. Because our vertex buffer is an array of vertices, rather than separate arrays of points, colors, and normals, the calls to *VertexAttribPointer* must change. In particular, the *stride* is changed from 0 to *sizeof(Vertex)* and the offset becomes an offset into the *Vertex* structure.

Because a vertex is repeated for each of its impinging faces, no index array is created and the call to *glDrawElements* is replaced with a call to *glDrawArrays*:

```
glUseProgram(program);
VertexAttribPointer(program, "point", 3,
        sizeof(Vertex), (void *) 0);                  // no skip
VertexAttribPointer(program, "color", 3,
        sizeof(Vertex), (void *) (sizeof(vec3));      // skip point
VertexAttribPointer(program, "normal", 3,
        sizeof(Vertex), (void *) (2*sizeof(vec3))); // skip point, color
SetUniform(program, "modelview", camera.modelview);
SetUniform(program, "persp", camera.persp);
SetUniform(program, "lightVec", vec3(.7f, .4f, -.2f));
glDrawArrays(GL_QUADS, 0, sizeof(vertices)/sizeof(Vertex));
```

In this section faceted shading was achieved through a duplication of vertices. We will see in chapter 15 (meshes) that this technique supports faceted/smooth combinations. We will also see a simpler method for faceted-only shading.

For a (mostly) smooth object like the VW Beetle, a faceted appearance is objectionable. Its remedy is *smooth shading*, which is described in the next chapter.

9.3 Exercise

Apply the modifications in the previous section to the previous exercise to produce a faceted cube. It's easier to utilize the full viewport.

Bonus 1

Like the previous exercise (sec. 7.6) that split the screen left/right, display the colorful cube on the left and the faceted cube on the right.

This can be accomplished with a test in the pixel shader:

```
uniform int colorfulShade;  // 0 for false, 1 for true
. . .
if (colorfulShade == 1) { . . . }
else { . . . }
```

Alternatively, one can create two shader programs using the same pixel shader, but different vertex shaders. (Multiple shader programs are sometimes preferable to a single but overly complicated shader.)

progColorful = LinkProgramViaCode(&vertexColorfulShader, &pixelShader);
progGouraud = LinkProgramViaCode(&vertexFacetShader, &pixelShader);

Use a different viewport for each shader program; the same call to *glDrawArrays* can be made for both viewports. Switch between shader programs with *glUseProgram*.

Bonus 2

Create a flat, shaded cube such as the following. Where in the code is this easiest to achieve?

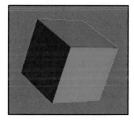

Figure 9-6: Flat-shaded cube

84

Chapter 10: Smooth Shading

For a surface that is primarily smooth, like the VW Beetle, the faceted appearance of figure 9.3 is objectionable. In 1971, Henri Gouraud, using a hardware rasterizer developed the previous year by Gary Watkins, introduced *smooth* (or *Gouraud*) *shading*.

The Watkins device performed bilinear interpolation, scan line by scan line (see section 4.2), to compute x' and z' for the visible portions of a polygon. It could also interpolate additional, arbitrary values (this is true of a modern rasterizer; e.g., in exercise 4.5, the rasterizer interpolates color).

Gouraud used a Lambert reflection model to compute a shaded value for each mesh vertex; the results were sent to the rasterizer. Of the final image he wrote, "visual discontinuities between adjacent polygons disappear, thus restoring the apparent smoothness of the surface and increasing greatly the realism of the pictures produced."

Figure 10-2: Smooth shaded Beetle, Henri Gouraud
(used with permission)

With bilinear interpolation, adjacent polygons that share vertex attributes will be continuous in color, texture, and surface normal along their common edge. If the normal field is smooth, as, e.g., below, then so will be the shading across polygons.

Figure 10-1: A smooth normal field

Unfortunately, Gouraud shading can exhibit artifacts. For example, depending on the illumination model, a highlight in the middle of a polygon is severely attenuated by the bilinear interpolation if it doesn't also appear at a polygon vertex.

And, although the shading values are continuous across an edge, their gradients are not. This results in an artifact akin to the Mach band effect in which a barely perceived brightness appears. Below, the green arrow points to a slender, vertical, bright artifact. It is readily perceived on a computer monitor but less noticeable on the printed page.

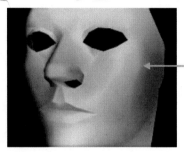

Figure 10-3: Faceted and smooth shading with visual artifacts
(courtesy Henri Gouraud)

To eliminate the gradient discontinuity, Gouraud proposed a cubic interpolant. This was not implemented, however, as the hardware was limited to linear interpolation.

10.1 Phong Shading

In 1973, Bui Tuong Phong resolved the Gouraud artifacts by using the rasterizer to interpolate the vertex normal, not the vertex shade. The interpolated normal must then be re-normalized (set to unit length) and used to compute the pixel shade. This approach is known as *Phong shading*.

Phong improved on specular highlights by explicitly calculating R, the light vector reflected about the normal. If the eye were in the direction R from the surface represented by the pixel (for an ideal reflective surface), then it would be exposed most directly to the highlight. So Phong used the angle between the eye vector E and the reflected vector R to compute the specular component.

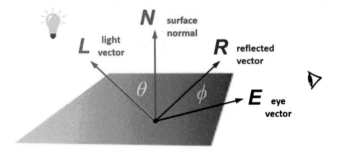

$$I = a + d\, \mathbf{L} \cdot \mathbf{N} + s\, (\mathbf{R} \cdot \mathbf{E})^k = a + d\, \cos(\theta) + s\, \cos(\phi)^k$$

Figure 10-4: Geometry of Phong lighting

When the Phong lighting model is combined with the Phong shading model, the results are significantly improved compared with Gouraud shading. In the figure below, the resolutions of the spheres are the same (as can be seen by the silhouette edges).

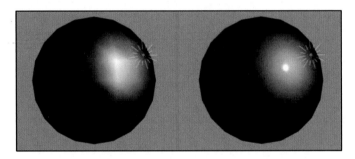

Figure 10-5: Comparison Gouraud (left) and Phong (right) shading

These early shading models distinguished between a diffuse color C_d, namely the color of the surface, and a specular color C_s, typically the color of the light. Thus, the previous equation can be rewritten to compute a final color C:

$$C = a\, C_a + d\, \cos(\theta)\, C_d + s\, \cos(\phi)^k\, C_s$$

where a, d, and s are coefficients selected by the programmer or user.

Real-time application of Phong's method exceeded the ability of most graphics hardware before 2000; until then Gouraud shading had been standard practice for interactive applications.

Figure 10-6: Bui Tuong Phong
(courtesy F. Crow)

In his 1976 dissertation, Jim Blinn improved shading through consideration of micro-geometry. In the early eighties, Rob Cook studied the subtleties in computing a final color. Additional shading developments include soft shadows, effects of global illumination, sub-surface light scattering, radiosity and more. They each improve the realism of a shaded scene. But for many applications, the Phong shading described in this chapter proves satisfactory.

10.2 Exercise: a Phong-Shaded Face

In this exercise we'll recreate the early work of Gouraud by digitizing a human face.

We'll modify CubeColorGouraud (renaming it to FacePhong) so that it
1) uses the shape of a face, not a cube,
2) implements smooth, not faceted, shading, and
3) implements Phong lighting (that is, a more realistic highlight) and Phong shading (that is, interpolating the surface normal at the pixel level).

Mark and Photograph the Face

For this exercise it is useful to work in pairs: one person the painter, the other the paintee.

1) Painter: photograph a full-face image of the paintee, for later use (chapter 12) as a *texture map*.

2) Painter: apply eyeliner to the paintee, à la Sylvie Gouraud, below; especially, increase detail near the eyes, lips, and nose. Just mark the left or right half of the face; you can

then render just the half, or reflect it for a full face. If reflecting, the straighter is the center-line, the better.

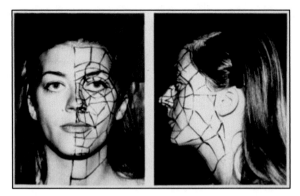

Figure 10-7: Sylvie Gouraud with lined face
(used with permission)

3) Take full-face and profile pictures, keeping the two close in scale.

4) Carefully remove the eyeliner.

Label the Pictures

Transfer the three images (full-face before painting, full-face and profile after painting) to a computer.

Label each vertex in the painted images with an identifying index (it may be easier to print the images first, labelling the vertices with pen or pencil).

Start your indexing at 0. Be certain the indices used in profile correspond with those in full-face. Figure 10-7 has about 80 vertices.

Define Vertices

Create a points list for the vertices:

```
vec3 points[] = {
   vec3(x0, y0, z0),
   vec3(x1, y1, z1),
   . . .
   vec3(xn, yn, zn)
};
```
or
```
float points[] = {
   {x0, y0, z0},
   {x1, y1, z1},
   . . .
   {xn, yn, zn}
};
```

89

Obtain *x* and *y* coordinates from the full-face image and *z*-coordinates from the profile:

   a) read the pictures into a paint program and obtain coordinates from the cursor, or
   b) print the pictures and measure coordinates with a ruler

It will prove convenient if the points are scaled and offset so their coordinates are within +/-1. This can be done with:

```
include <float.h>

void Normalize() {
  int npoints = sizeof(points)/sizeof(vec3);
  // scale and offset so that points all within +/-1 in x, y, and z
  vec3 mn(FLT_MAX), mx(-FLT_MAX);
  for (int i = 0; i < npoints; i++) {
      vec3 p = points[i];
      for (int k = 0; k < 3; k++) {
          if (p[k] < mn[k]) mn[k] = p[k];
          if (p[k] > mx[k]) mx[k] = p[k];
      }
  }
  vec3 center = .5f*(mn+mx), range = mx-mn;
  float maxrange = max(range.x, max(range.y, range.z));
  float s = 2/maxrange;
  for (int i = 0; i < npoints; i++)
      points[i] = s*(points[i]-center);
}
```

Define Triangles/Quadrilaterals

Number the triangles/quadrilaterals on the images. Then, create a list of triangles and/or a list of quadrilaterals for use with *glDrawElements*.

Even though we are unable to draw lines across the eyes and lips, attempt to define a triangulation over them.

Triangle Orientation

Care must be taken that the triangles are properly *oriented* in the *triangles* array. By OpenGL convention, a triangle (or quad) that appears connected in *counter-clockwise* order when viewed from outside is *forward-facing*, with the surface normal facing the viewer.

The subroutine *cross* in VecMat.h is a *right-handed* cross product; for a triangle whose vertices *v1*, *v2*, and *v3* appear CCW, cross(v2-v1, v3-v2) will face the viewer. If the vertices are listed in clock-wise order, the resulting triangle normal will face away.

In the following section we compute surface normals for each vertex by averaging the triangle normals surrounding the vertex. If the triangles are not consistently oriented, the average of triangle surface normals can be wildly inaccurate, as shown below.

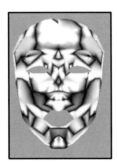

Figure 10-8: Bad surface normals from inconsistently oriented triangles

Compute Surface Normals

With a smooth mesh, vertex attributes (point, color, normal, and/or texture) are shared with those faces (triangles or quads) that surround the vertex.

If unknown, a vertex normal can be approximated as the average of surface normals of those facets that surround the vertex. If the geometry is meant to contain creases, however, the resulting normals may be inappropriate.

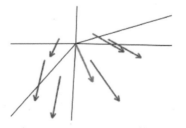

Figure 10-9: The vertex normal (green) as average of surrounding triangle normals (red)

This is implemented for triangles by the following:

```
// declare array of normals, one for each point
const int npoints = sizeof(points)/sizeof(int);
vec3 normals[npoints];
```

Now, initialize the array and set the normals:

```
// zero array
for (int i = 0; i < npoints; i++)
    normals[i] = vec3(0, 0, 0);
// compute normal for each triangle, accumulate for each vertex
for (int i = 0; i < ntriangles; i++) {
    int *t = triangles[i];
    vec3 p1(points[t[0]]), p2(points[t[1]]), p3(points[t[2]]);
    vec3 n = normalize(cross(p3-p2, p2-p1));
    for (int k = 0; k < 3; k++)
        normals[t[k]] += n;
}
// set vertex normals to unit length
for (int i = 0; i < npoints; i++)
    normals[i] = normalize(normals[i]);
```

Changes to InitVertexBuffer

In *InitVertexBuffer* the points and normals must be copied to a GPU vertex buffer:

```
void InitVertexBuffer() {
    // create GPU buffer, make it the active buffer
    glGenBuffers(1, &vBuffer);
    glBindBuffer(GL_ARRAY_BUFFER, vBuffer);
    // allocate memory for vertex positions and normals
    int sizePts = sizeof(points), sizeNms = sizeof(normals);
    glBufferData(GL_ARRAY_BUFFER, sizePts+sizeNms, NULL, GL_STATIC_DRAW);
    // copy data
    glBufferSubData(GL_ARRAY_BUFFER, 0, sizePts, &points[0]);
    glBufferSubData(GL_ARRAY_BUFFER, sizePts, sizeNrms, &normals[0]);
}
```

Changes to the Vertex Shader

Gouraud shading computes intensities (i.e., the diffuse and specular colors) in the vertex shader and interpolates them in the rasterizer; Phong shading is more realistic because the rasterizer interpolates a geometric entity, the surface normal, and the pixel shader computes the intensity.

We simplify the application by not supporting color as a vertex attribute (we'll reintroduce it in chapter 12, as *texture*). The vertex shader still takes a normal and point as input, but color is no longer stored in the buffer or sent to the vertex shader. With this exercise we'll produce a black & white (i.e., "grayscale") image.

The pixel shader will perform the shading, so the calculation of *d* and *s*, done by the vertex shader in the previous exercise, must be moved to the pixel shader.

The default ambient term should also be moved to the pixel shader:

```
uniform float a = .2;
```

The vertex shader must still transform the input normal and input point:

```
out vec3 vPoint;
out vec3 vNormal;
vPoint = (modelview*vec4(point, 1)).xyz;
vNormal = (modelview*vec4(normal, 0)).xyz;
gl_Position = persp*vec4(vPoint, 1);
```

The results are now passed to the pixel shader *vPoint* and *vNormal*:

Changes to the Pixel Shader

The pixel shader now takes a surface normal and a position as input:

```
in vec3 vPoint;
in vec3 vNormal;
```

To emphasize the quality of Phong shading, we'll use a *local light*, rather than the infinite light used for the color cube. To do this, replace the uniform *lightVec* with the following input for the pixel shader:

```
uniform vec3 lightPos = vec3(1,0,0); // 3D light location w/ default
```

Colors are no longer sent to the pixel shader from the vertex shader, but we can provide a default color as a uniform input to the pixel shader:

```
uniform vec3 color = vec3(1, 1, 1);  // default is white
```

The pixel shader receives an interpolated surface normal. Because these interpolations do not produce unit length vectors, the incoming *vNormal* must be set to unit-length (*normalize* is a built-in function of GLSL):

```
vec3 N = normalize(vNormal);              // unit-length surface normal
```

The light vector must be computed from the light position and the input point:

```
vec3 L = normalize(lightPos-vPoint);      // light vector
```

The diffuse calculation is moved from the vertex shader to the pixel shader:

```
float d = abs(dot(N, L));                 // two-sided diffuse
```

With Phong shading, the specular coefficient depends on a highlight term that is computed by applying Lambert's law to the eye vector E and the reflected light vector R (see figure 10-4).

Recall that L is the (unit-length) light vector (direction from the pixel's point in space to the light source) and that N is the (unit-length) surface normal at the point. The vector R is the reflection of the light vector L around the surface normal N.

GLSL provides a built-in *reflect* function, so we can compute R as:

```
vec3 R = reflect(L, N);                   // reflected light vector
```

R is unit-length (L already is, and reflection does not change vector length).

The "eye" vector E is the unit-length direction from the surface point to the eye (camera). Recall in camera space that the eye (camera) is at the origin, so E is simply:

```
vec3 E = normalize(vPoint);               // eye vector
```

The highlight h, specular reflection s, and *intensity* can now be computed; the pixel value is then output:

```
float h = max(0, dot(R, E));              // highlight term
float s = pow(h, 100);                    // specular term
float intensity = clamp(a+d+s, 0, 1);
pColor = vec4(intensity*color, 1);
```

Changes to *Display*

The vertex fetch instructions must now be for point and normal, but not color:

94

```
VertexAttribPointer(program, "point", 3, 0, (void *) 0);
VertexAttribPointer(program, "normal", 3, 0,  (void *) sizePts);
```

Unlike with the cube, the face should be rendered with *glDrawElements*.

Bonus

Within your application, create a reflected set of vertices for a complete, symmetric face. `To prevent a crease in the middle of the face, do not duplicate the center (left-to-right) vertices.

Figure 10-10: Crease due to mid-line vertex duplication

Comment

If the grayscale results are discouraging, consider we're more than half way towards figure 15-2.

Chapter 11: Widgets

The previous chapters have allowed us to produce some simple images of 3D objects. Before examining more advanced methods of display, let's pause to consider how the user might interact with the scene.

The Widgets library supports several user interface operations. These include 'direct manipulation' of 3D geometric entities, that is, moving or orienting a 3D entity given 2D mouse input superimposed on the object. Implementation details are in Widget.cpp, but brief descriptions of the principal functions are given here.

11.1 Picking

Selection is a basic operation for interactive computer graphics. Given the cursor location, selection of a point from a collection of points can be done in screen-space; that is, after a vertex is transformed to the screen, its distance to the cursor can be tested. But this hinders selection of a primitive (i.e., triangle) or a location within a primitive.

It is, therefore, advantageous to regard the cursor as on a 3D line viewed end-on. Vertex selection then becomes a 3D test for proximity to the line and primitive selection becomes a test for primitive/line intersection.

In later chapters we consider two examples (20-Example-MeshTessTexture.cpp for selection with a mesh and 20-Example-BallTessQuad for selection with a sphere). *RaySphere* is found in Misc.cpp and *IntersectWithLine* is found in Mesh.cpp. Both subroutines rely on the subroutine *ScreenLine* (found in Draw.cpp), which we consider briefly.

ScreenLine

Given a screen location (in pixels), *ScreenLine* computes two 3D points that represent a line that, when transformed by the camera's view, runs through the given pixel, perpendicular to the screen.

This requires defining two points, each with the same pixel (x, y), but with different (and arbitrary) z-values. By transforming both of these device-space points by the inverse of the camera transformation, a 3D line in camera-space is obtained. The actual matrix inversion and transformation are performed by *gluUnProject*, a subroutine from the GL utility interface, glu.h. (Additional inverse transformations can take the line to world space or to object space.)

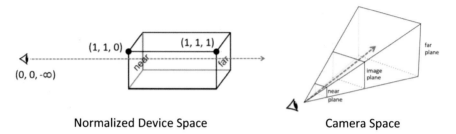

Normalized Device Space   Camera Space

Figure 11-1: Inverse transform of two points in NDS to Eye Space

Once a 3D line is defined, it can, for example, be tested for intersection against the triangles defining a mesh. Or, once a point is chosen, it could be used as a new center of rotation.

11.2 Mover

The user may wish to move a point, such as the light source or a corner of a triangle. Widget.cpp implements the Mover class, which allows a point to be moved in a plane perpendicular to the view direction. This produces a reasonably intuitive motion.

When the point is selected, a plane is computed that has a surface normal equal to the camera's line of sight, passing through the selected point. The camera's line of sight is determined by transforming the negative z-axis by the inverse *modelview* matrix.

Upon mouse drag, *ScreenLine* computes a line given the cursor and the dragged point is positioned at the intersection of the line with the previously computed plane. The line is determined by a single point on the screen as well as the origin inverse-transformed by the *modelview* matrix.

11.3 Aimer

We can augment the mover with an ability to aim. The Aimer class defines a virtual sphere that, given a mouse location, determines direction. This can be useful for certain tasks, but quaternions are a more general means to specify orientation (see chapter 22).

11.4 Whence and Whither

The arrow is often used to represent a vector, such as a surface normal.

If the base and head of the arrow are 2D points, the arrow can be drawn as a connecting shaft and a fixed-angle 'V' located at the head and centered on the shaft, regardless of shaft direction. The arrow is drawn as three, 2D lines.

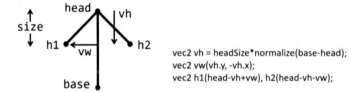

vec2 vh = headSize*normalize(base-head);
vec2 vw(vh.y, -vh.x);
vec2 h1(head-vh+vw), h2(head-vh-vw);

Figure 11-2: A two-dimensional arrow

If the endpoints are 3D and the depth buffer is used, the arrow should be drawn as three, 3D lines, to allow for depth testing. But it must maintain its 2D appearance. Details may be found in the subroutine Draw::ArrowV. With some small effort, it determines 3D points that are transformed by the camera to the 2D points *h1* and *h2*.

11.5 Magnifier

There are occasions when one wishes to closely inspect an image. A number of magnified images are presented in chapter 13, for example. A common technique is to display a pixel as a large square. Although not a theoretically correct representation, it is useful and typical of a magnifier.

Figure 11-3: A magnified view

A magnifier that can inspect any part of the entire computer screen is not easily implemented (several are available for download). But a magnifier for use within an application is relatively simple to implement with OpenGL; the details are in Widget.cpp. The application need only define the tool:

Magnifier magnifier(int2(xSource, ySource), int2(xDispSize, yDispSize), pSize);

This establishes the initial location (within the application's window) to read pixels from the display. The size of the magnified display is set to (*xDispSize*, *yDispSize*) and the scale of the magnified pixel is set to *pSize*. The number of pixels displayed is determined by these three sizes.

The magnifier is displayed by a call to *Magnifier::Display*, specifying the location of the magnified sub-window.

The source location can be interactively specified if mouse handlers are connected to the magnifier's *Down* and *Drag* routines. The scale of the magnifier, *magnifier.blockSize*, can be also be set by the application. Example magnifier use is in 20-Demo-BezierLOD.cpp and 20-Example-MeshTessTexture.cpp.

11.6 Exercise: Lights! Action!

Beginning with the previous exercise in Phong shading (10.2), let's use the *Mover* class to interactively position the light source.

In addition to the *Mover* class from Widgets, we'll also use the Draw library; include statements for these headers are needed by the application.

A local, default light should be defined at the top of the application:

```
vec3 lightSource(1.7f, 1.1f, 1.3f);
```

The uniform *lightPos* should already be defined as an input to the pixel shader. And, as in the previous exercise, the light location is transformed by *modelview* and then sent to the pixel shader, in *Display*:

```
vec4 hLight = camera.modelview*vec4(lightSource, 1);
SetUniform(program, "lightPos", (vec3 *) &hLight);
```

At the end of *Display*, we represent the light source by calling the *Disk* subroutine in Draw. Draw.cpp has its own shader program, which should first be selected:

```
UseDrawShader(camera.fullview);
Disk(lightSource, 12, vec3(1,0,0));
```

After the declaration of *lightSource*, but before the declaration of our mouse callbacks, we need two variables to control the motion of the light:

```
Mover    mover;          // to reposition light source
void     *picked = NULL;  // camera or light selected?
```

Mover repositions lightSource in response to a mouse-drag, assuming the light has first been selected.

After the above declarations, the only changes needed are to the mouse callbacks; *MouseButton* and *MouseMove* need to call *lightMover* subroutines.

The *Mover* routines work with OpenGL routines that define the screen space origin at the *lower* left of the application window. The operating system, however, probably defines the origin to be *upper* left. For programming, it is convenient to invert the mouse *y*-coordinate.

To do this, one must know the window height:

```
int WindowHeight(GLFWwindow *w) {
    int width, height;
    glfwGetWindowSize(w, &width, &height);
    return height;
}
```

Then, in both *MouseButton* and *MouseMove*, the sense of *y* is inverted by:

```
y = WindowHeight(w)-y;
```

The *MouseButton* routine must first determine whether the light source has been selected, or (alternatively) the user is modifying the camera:

```
picked = NULL;
if (action == GLFW_PRES) {
    if (MouseOver(x, y, lightSource, camera.fullview)) {
        // MouseOver in Widget.h
        picked = &lightSource;
        lightMover.Down(picked, x, y, camera.modelview, camera.persp);
    }
    else {
        picked = &camera;
        camera.MouseDown(x, y);
    }
}
```

Finally, the *MouseMove* routine drags the light or camera, depending on *picked*:

```
if (picked == &lightSource)
    mover.Drag(x, y, camera.modelview, camera.persp);
if (picked == &camera)
    camera.MouseDrag(x, y, shift);
```

Bonus: Multiple Lights

To achieve good lighting often requires a large number of lights. Suppose we wish to extend the light source by defining multiple lights:

The *MouseButton* routine must test the lights for selection:

```
for (size_t i = 0; i < lights.size(); i++)
    if (::MouseOver(x, y, lights[i].p, fullview, xCursorOffset, yCursorOffset)) {
        picked = &lights[i];
        mover.Down(&(*l).p, x, y, modelview, persp);
    }
```

The display subroutine transforms the lights by the camera's *modelview* and sends them to the pixel shader:

```
vec3 xlights[4];
for (int i = 0; i < nlights; i++) {
    vec4 xl(camera.modelview*vec4(lights[i], 1));
    xlights[i] = vec3(xl.x, xl.y, xl.z);
}
SetUniform3v(program, "lights", nlights, &xlights[0].x);
```

```
      SetUniform3v(program, "lightColors", nlights, &lightColors[0].x);
```
The pixel shader can declare an array of uniforms for the light positions and colors:

```
    uniform int nlights;
    uniform vec3 lights[20];
    uniform vec3 lightColors[20];
```

It then computes total diffuse intensity of a surface color, and accumulates the specular highlight colors:

```
    float a = .15, d = 0;
    vec3 specColor;
    vec3 N = normalize(normal);
    vec3 E = -normalize(gPt);
    bool sideViewer = dot(E, N) < 0;
    // compute total diffuse & specular intensities
    float intensity = .2;
    for (int i = 0; i < nlights; i++) {
        vec3 L = normalize(lights[i]-gPt);
        bool sideLight = dot(L, N) < 0;
        if (sideLight == sideViewer) {
            d += max(0, dot(N, L));
            vec3 R = reflect(L, N);          // highlight vector
            float h = max(0, dot(R, E));     // highlight term
            float s = pow(h, 50);            // specular term
            specColor += s*lightColors[i];   // accumulate spec. color
        }
    }
    float ad = clamp(a+d, 0, 1);
    pColor = vec4(ad*vec3(1,1,1)+specColor, 1);
```

Chapter 12: Texture Mapping

12.1 Pixel Modulation

The intensity of a shaded pixel can be modulated by an arbitrary 'texture'. In OpenGL, multiple texture images may be applied, and an image may represent semi-transparent as well as opaque texture. The technique was first implemented by Ed Catmull, who credited Lance Williams with the concept.

Figure 12-1: First texture-mapped images, 1974
(used with permission)

Traditionally, texture mapping is defined in two-dimensions as a rectangular image ("solid texture" is defined in three dimensions, but is not considered here), defined over a rectangular domain (0, 1) X (0, 1) with texture position given by (u, v).

12.2 Mapping between Object and Texture

The texture map is associated with a triangle or quad according to the *texture coordinates* of its vertices. These coordinates are specified as a (u, v) pair.

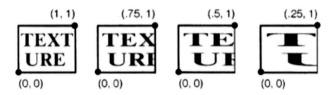

Figure 12-2: Effect of changing texture coordinates

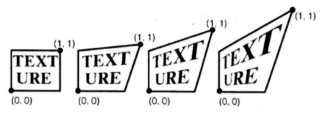

Figure 12-3: Effect of changing shape

The stretching above is represented in a continuous space. In reality, texture mapping *samples* a *discrete texture map* at intervals that depend on pixel-to-pixel spacing. Pixels in a straight line in screen space remain in a straight line in texture space, although their footprint and spacing changes along the line.

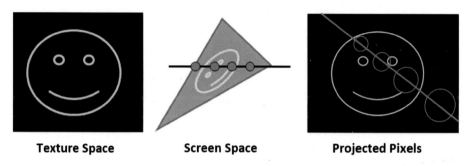

Texture Space   **Screen Space**   **Projected Pixels**

Figure 12-4: Pixel spacing with respect to texture

12.3 Mesh Texture

In the teacup below, the vertices are mostly smooth-shaded and continuous. But there are discontinuities in surface normal and texture along the perimeter of the base (blue circle), allowing the teacup base and the teacup wall to have different appearances.

As discussed in section 9.2, the points along the perimeter must appear twice in the GPU buffer: once for the teacup wall in which surface normals point outwards and once for the teacup base in which surface normals point downwards.

The duplicated vertex has the same location but a different surface normal. Also, it is assigned different texture coordinates. Along the bottom edge, the (u, v) pairs for the wall trace out a line in texture space; the (u, v) pairs for the base trace out a circle in texture space.

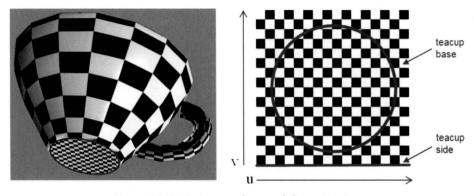

Figure 12-5: Texture and normal discontinuity

Multiple textures can be defined by a single texture image (a.k.a. an *atlas*). The initial assignment of *u,v* coordinates to vertices and/or 'texture painting' can be made with freeware like *Blender*.

Figure 12-6: Multiple Textures
(model and texture courtesy TurboSquid)

12.4 Exercise: Textured Triangle

In this exercise we'll map a 2D image onto a triangle.

Neither OpenGL nor GLFW (version 3) provide access to raster image files (the application frameworks SDL and Qt do support several raster formats). There are several popular image formats, and the content varies in terms of encoding and ancillary information (such as photometry).

We'll use Misc.h to read Targa files. The format is simple, and there are numerous free viewing programs that will write a .targa file.

OpenGL uses the term "texture" to refer to any map (the typical texture map described in this chapter as well as the bump map and displacement map described in later chapters). Within the shaders, an individual map is referred to as a "sampler2D".

At the top of our application we can define a single triangle of three points and three *uv texture coordinates*. The range of the texture coordinates suggests the upper left triangular half of the texture image will cover the triangle.

```
float pts[][3] = {{-.4f, -.5f, 0}, {-.1f, .8f, 0}, {.6f, -.5f, 0}};
float uvs[][2] = {{0, 0}, {0, 1}, {1, 1}}; // lo-left,up-left,up-right

void InitVertexBuffer() {
  glGenBuffers(1, &vBuffer);
  glBindBuffer(GL_ARRAY_BUFFER, vBuffer);
  int sizePts = sizeof(points), sizeUvs = sizeof(uvs);
  glBufferData(GL_ARRAY_BUFFER, sizePts+sizeUvs, NULL, GL_STATIC_DRAW);
  glBufferSubData(GL_ARRAY_BUFFER, 0, sizePts, &points[0]);
  glBufferSubData(GL_ARRAY_BUFFER, sizePts, sizeNrms, &uvs[0]);
}
```

Initialize the Texture Map

Texture-related OpenGL subroutines need two identifiers: a *texture name* that is provided by OpenGL and a *texture unit* that is assigned by the programmer. The texture unit refers to a physical buffer in the GPU, and the application can freely assign a value.

LoadTexture is a convenience routine in the Misc library that reads a Targa file and sets the texture name (with a call to *glGenTextures*). The name (an integer identifier) is used as an argument to *glBindTexture* and *glDeleteBuffers*.

The application should set the texture unit, and then initialize the texture name:

```
int textureUnit = 0;
GLuint textureName = LoadTexture(filename, textureUnit); // in Misc.h
```

The application's *Display* establishes access to the texture map. The texture unit is needed to specify a shader's current sampler2D (i.e., which texture map in memory), and it is also an argument to *glActiveTexture*:

```
glActiveTexture(GL_TEXTURE0+textureUnit);
glBindTexture(GL_TEXTURE_2D, textureName);
SetUniform(program, "textureImage", textureUnit);
```

106

Display also establishes the vertex fetch:

```
VertexAttribPointer(prog, "pt", 3, 0, (void *) 0);
VertexAttribPointer(prog,"uv", 2, 0, (void*) sizeof(pts));
```

Changes to the Shaders

The vertex shader still accepts a *vec3 point* and transforms it by the view matrix, but it needs a new input and output for the texture coordinates:

```
in vec2 uv;
out vec2 vuv;
```

The *uv* coordinates are simply passed through by the vertex shader, to be interpolated by the rasterizer:

```
vuv = uv;
```

The pixel shader can now use the texture map. It requires an input for *uv* coordinates, and a uniform to access the map:

```
in vec2 vuv;
uniform sampler2D textureImage;
```

The pixel shader sets its output to be the value of the texture map at the given *uv*:

```
vec4 texColor = texture(textureImage, vuv); // includes alpha
pColor = vec4(texColor.rgb, 1);             // but make opaque
```

The result should appear similar to:

Figure 12-7: A textured triangle

Multiple Colored Lights and Texture

The use of texture allows us to see the effect of colored lights when they are applied to specular reflection, but not diffuse reflection (as described in the previous chapter).

In the following image, left, a cube is rendered with texture and colored highlights. The light sources are shown as small circles. The same cube is shown without highlights, center, and without texture, right.

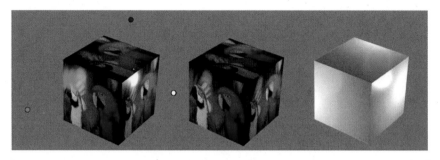

Figure 12-8: A textured cube with multiple lights

Chapter 13: Anti-Aliasing

13.1 Artifice and Artifact

The previous chapters have described the basic methods behind the magic of computer graphics. The code of secrecy requires a magician not to reveal the artifice behind an illusion. In computer graphics, the artifice is rasterization. If we are not careful, it is revealed as *aliasing*, an undesired artifact sometimes called "the jaggies".

Frank Crow provided the first analysis of aliasing in computer graphics, describing the conditions that cause moiré patterns, small details disappearing, and staircased edges. Although these are less troubling with increased display resolutions, they remain of fundamental concern to computer graphics.

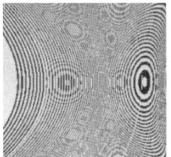  

Figure 13-1: Images with aliasing; Frank Crow
(used with permission)

There are many anti-aliasing methods, of varied sophistication. OpenGL provides three that are easy to apply: super-sampling (a.k.a. multi-sampling), coverage blending, and mipmapping.

13.2 Super-Sampling

If we consider the triangle in chapter 4, its edges appear staircased. This is because a pixel is set to one of only two values: the color of the triangle or the background color. The staircasing can be reduced if the pixel value is a blend of these two colors. A simple means to achieve this is with *super-sampling*, in which the value of a pixel is determined through the averaging of *sub-pixels*.

In the magnification below, at left is a conventionally rendered edge; those pixels within the triangle, signified by a green dot, are shaded red, those outside (black dot) are shaded blue. At right, for each pixel computed by the pixel shader, four separate *sub-pixels* are written into an increased-sized memory. The method does not increase the number of calls to the pixel shader, but uses a higher resolution depth buffer to estimate pixel coverage (e.g., for a pixel inside a triangle, coverage is 100%, but along an edge, with four sub depth-pixels, the coverage can be 0, 25, 50, or 75, or 100 per cent.

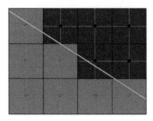 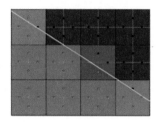

Figure 13-2: Effect of super-sampling on edge

When all the sub-pixels have been written, OpenGL writes into the actual display raster an average of the triangle and background colors based on the sub-pixel coverage. This has no effect inside the triangle, but along its edges the averaging substantially reduces the staircasing.

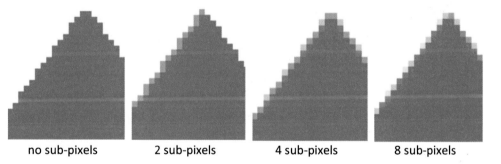

| no sub-pixels | 2 sub-pixels | 4 sub-pixels | 8 sub-pixels |

Figure 13-3: Super-sampling

OpenGL supports 2, 4, or 8 sub-pixels. This requires a commensurate increase in z-buffer memory, and may not be supported by all hardware. A framework (GLFW) call is recommended over low-level calls to OpenGL. The following sets super-sampling to 4; it should precede the call to *glfwCreateWindow*:

```
glfwWindowHint(GLFW_SAMPLES, 4); // supersamping, 4 sub-pixels
```

110

13.3 Coverage Blending: Smooth Lines

In chapter 7 we displayed a cube with lines. If the image is rendered with super-sampling (chapter 4), the aliasing is reduced.

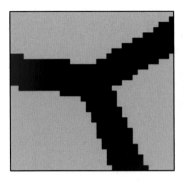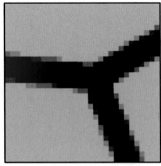

Figure 13-4: Left: without super-sampling; right: super-sampled, 4 sub-pixels

OpenGL offers an additional method to render a line smoothly, by blending background and line color based on coverage of a pixel by the line. The rasterizer multiplies the coverage of a pixel (i.e., 100% for an internal pixel, < 100% for an edge pixel) by the alpha (opacity) returned by the pixel shader. Pixel coverage by a line can be accurately computed, so this blend method improves over super-sampling.

Figure 13-5: Coverage blended

To invoke this blending, at the beginning of *Display*, add:

```
glDisable(GL_MULTISAMPLE); // else multisample overrides blend
glEnable(GL_BLEND);
glBlendFunc(GL_SRC_ALPHA, GL_ONE_MINUS_SRC_ALPHA);
glEnable(GL_LINE_SMOOTH);
```

To re-establish super-sampling, simply

```
glEnable(GL_MULTISAMPLE);
```

The same blending can be applied to triangles and quads, if GL_POLYGON_SMOOTH is enabled. This will improve silhouette edges but will also introduce artifacts along internal mesh edges. And so, coverage blending is not recommended for triangles or quads.

Round Ends

Lines are drawn by default with square ends. To round the ends of a line, a circular disk can be drawn at each endpoint. This can be done with coverage blending, first by enabling point blending and then rendering each vertex as a point:

```
glEnable(GL_POINT_SMOOTH);
glDisable(GL_MULTISAMPLE);
glPointSize(pixelDiameter);
glDrawArrays(GL_POINTS, 0, npoints);
```

This may not work for OpenGL v3 and above, however. An alternative is found in *Draw::Disk*.

13.4 Anti-Aliased Texture

OpenGL offers a third anti-aliasing method, specific to texture maps. The previous two techniques (super-sampling, which improves the quality of the silhouette edge, and coverage blending, which improves the quality of a line) have little effect on texture. Texture quality is determined by whether the texture map is properly *filtered*.

Consider the teacup from the previous chapter. Given an oblique view of its side and bottom, the chessboard squares appear ragged. That is, the pixel obtains a value from a single point on the chessboard texture, which is either black or white, but not gray.

```
pColor = vec4(texture(textureImage, vuv).rgb, 1);
```

112

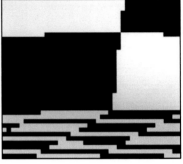

Figure 13-6: Teacup with aliased texture

As with edge staircasing, the solution involves averaging. If the pixel represents an average of some region of the chessboard, shades of gray will appear. The simplest average is bilinear interpolation of the four nearest texture pixels. It is computationally inexpensive and easily invoked with OpenGL:

```
glTexParameteri(GL_TEXTURE_2D, GL_TEXTURE_MIN_FILTER, GL_LINEAR);
glTexParameteri(GL_TEXTURE_2D, GL_TEXTURE_MAG_FILTER, GL_LINEAR);
```

(The interpolation can be disabled by passing **GL_NEAREST** rather **GL_LINEAR**.)

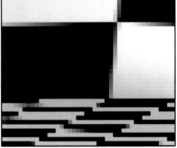

Figure 13-7: Teacup with bilinearly interpolated texture

This method provides modest improvement to the chessboard edges along the side of the teapot, where there are many pixels per chessboard square. But along the base of the teacup, where the distance between pixels increases in texture space and, thus, texture detail is overlooked, the image is still badly aliased.

The pixel rate along the bottom is insufficient and thus overlooks detail. Put another way, there must be a limit placed on the amount of detail in the object given a particular

113

pixel rate. Failure to properly limit the detail (i.e., before a GLSL call to *texture*) produces aliasing, i.e., scintillations, staircasing, and moiré patterns.

Given its importance, we take a moment to consider the theoretical underpinnings to anti-aliasing.

13.5 Digital Filtering

The texture image is an array of pixels, which is a two-dimensional *digital signal* that can be digitally filtered. A weighted average is a type of digital filter.

Example 2D filters are shown below. Each has a cross-sectional profile (called a *kernel*). The weights are symbolized by vertical red lines.

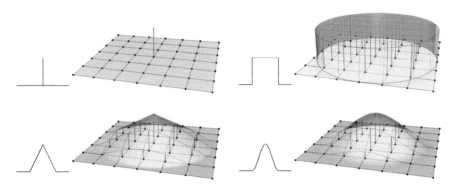

Figure 13-8: Filter kernel applied to texture pixels (blue grid)
top row: point sample and box filters, bottom: linear and cubic filters

To compute the weighted sum that corresponds with the center of the filter, each element of the filter multiplies its corresponding texture pixel value. The results are summed and normalized by the sum of all filter weights. This is a *convolution* of the filter with the texture image.

The shape of the filter kernel and its effect on reducing aliasing has received considerable study. The filter footprint is typically circular or, when the textured surface is not parallel to the screen, elliptical.

For example, consider the following image of a repeating texture. Four pixels, represented on the left by circles, are each centered at the base of the lily. These circles map to the texture as shown on the right. Because of the view angle, the nominally circular pixel footprint is elliptical in texture space.

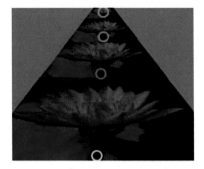 

Figure 13-9: Pixel footprints in texture space

Ideally, a pixel value is computed as a weighted average of those texture pixels within the corresponding ellipse. The cyan pixel, which is furthest, represents the largest texture region, one with considerable variation in color.

Of greater concern, however, is the size of the footprint: it should be at least twice the distance between pixels, such as in the figure below, where blue dots represent texture pixels and the red dots represent pixels in succession along a scan line.

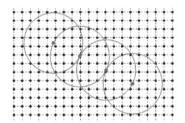

Figure 13-10: Pixels and their footprints mapped to texture image

That the footprint radius must equal or exceed the pixel-to-pixel distance is justified by a central pillar of signal processing, the *sampling theorem*. It is of fundamental significance to computer graphics.

13.6 The Sampling Theorem

In 1928, Harry Nyquist, an electrical engineer for A.T.T., concluded that the number of independent pulses that could be transmitted through a telegraph wire per unit time is limited to twice the bandwidth (i.e., highest frequency supported) of the wire.

Figure 13-11: Harry Nyquist and Claude Shannon

In 1949, Claude Shannon published what is considered the dual theory, often called the *Nyquist-Shannon sampling theorem*. It states that when sampling a signal, *the sampling rate must equal or exceed twice the signal's bandwidth*, i.e., its highest frequency. This condition is critical in bridging the continuous (analog) and discrete (digital) worlds without aliasing. It requires us to think of the texture map as a *digital signal*.

Let's consider a 1D example, below. A continuous signal (green) is sampled at regular intervals (vertical lines). The frequency of these samples is called the *sampling rate*. Half that rate is the *Nyquist frequency*. Central to the practice of sampling is the need, before the signal is sampled, to filter (remove) any frequencies in the original signal that are above the Nyquist frequency.

Put another way, if a signal is sampled at less than twice its bandwidth, aliasing will occur. The following figure provides two examples. A signal (in green) is sampled (red dots) and reconstructed (in blue). The sampling rate is 20 Hz. and the Nyquist frequency is 10 Hz. Both signals (18 Hz. and 14 Hz.) exceed the Nyquist frequency and the resulting reconstructions are aliased.

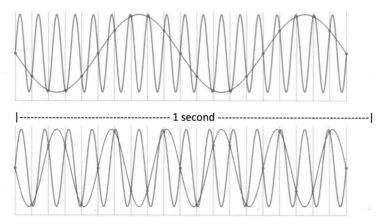

green: 18 Hz.
red: 20 Hz.
blue: 2 Hz.

|-------------------------------------- 1 second --------------------------------------|

green: 14 Hz.
red: 20 Hz.
blue: 6 Hz.

Figure 13-12: Aliasing (green signal, red samples, blue alias)

116

The frequency range from zero to the Nyquist frequency is known as the 'base band'. Frequencies above the Nyquist reflect back into the base band. If the signal is 18 Hz., it is 8 Hz. above the Nyquist frequency, and will reflect back to 8 Hz. below it, or 2 Hz. If the signal is 14 Hz., it is 4 above the Nyquist, and reflects back to 6 Hz.

Thus, the higher the frequency of the signal, the lower that of the alias, which accounts for the difference in aliasing between the side and bottom of the teacup: along the side there is some noticeable staircasing, but along the bottom, where pixel to pixel distance spans more of texture space, the chessboard pattern is severely degraded.

Texture mapping is a form of sampling in which the pixel spacing in screen space determines the sampling rate; the texture is a signal whose frequencies should not exceed half that rate. To eliminate aliasing, frequencies above the Nyquist frequency are removed, i.e., the signal is convolved with a *low-pass* kernel, as in section 13.4.

13.7 Mipmaps

The size and shape of the pixel footprint, in texture space, depend on pixel spacing and orientation with respect to the surface, both of which can change from pixel to pixel. To compute an elliptical weighted average for each pixel is computationally unsustainable at run-time. Rather, a pre-blurred texture image is typically used.

In 1983, Lance Williams developed a sequence of increasingly blurred textures, each half the size of its predecessor and ending with a single pixel. It is called a *mipmap* (*mip* for *multum in parvo*, or "much in little space").

Figure 13-13: A mipmap

OpenGL automatically selects the appropriate mipmap level for a pixel (determined from the change in *uv*-coordinates between adjacent pixels). Before OpenGLv3, one needed to build one's own set of maps, and then bundle them together as a mipmap. Since v3, one function achieves this: `glGenerateMipmap(GL_TEXTURE_2D);`

One can select a particular access of the mipmaps. The highest quality is obtained by a weighted average of the two nearest (i.e., bounding) mipmap levels, which is achieved with:

`glTexParameteri(GL_TEXTURE_2D, GL_TEXTURE_MIN_FILTER, GL_LINEAR_MIPMAP_LINEAR);`

 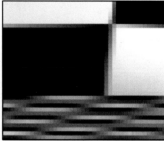

Figure 13-14: Teacup with anti-aliased texture

With mipmaps, an appropriately anti-aliased texture map is available regardless of the size of the pixel footprint when mapped to the original texture image.

As screen resolutions increase, aliasing will become less noticeable. But the techniques in this chapter remain important because aliasing is objectionable even in small amounts, and is often more apparent with animation.

Figure 13-15: Lance Williams
"The biggest screen is the one behind the eyes."

118

13.8 Exercises

A) Add super-sampling to ColorfulLetter (exercise 4.5). Use the Magnifier widget (or a zoom tool if you have one) to compare with and without aliasing.

B) Add blending for lines to CubePersp (chapter 7). Compare.

C) Compare texture mapping with mipmapping on/off. Mipmaps can be disabled in the pixel shader by replacing the call `texture(textureImage, teUv)` with `textureLod(textureImage, teUv, 0)`. Or, *LoadTexture* can be passed *mipmap* false.

Chapter 14: Bump Mapping

In 1978, Jim Blinn presented a technique to simulate wrinkled surfaces by modifying surface normals. The process, called *bump mapping*, significantly enhanced image realism. It provides the appearance of a bumpy surface without representing bumps geometrically (i.e., without additional vertices). In one approach, Blinn generated a field of surface normals from a *height field*.

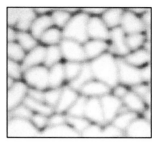

Figure 14-1: Bump-mapped orange and its height field; Jim Blinn
(used with permission)

The height field is a list of *z*-values over a (typically) rectangular grid in the *xy*-plane; the set of (x,y,z) defines a surface. It is often stored as a monochromatic image (or *depth map*) in which brightness represents height *z* and the pixel location represents *x* and *y*.

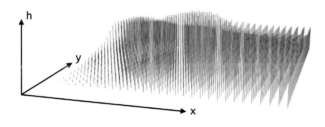

Figure 14-2: Depth map and heights above the *xy*-plane (red tallest, blue shortest)

14.1 Computing the Surface Normal from a Height Field

The height field is a function $h(x, y)$ whose partial derivatives in the *x* and *y* directions can be approximated with central differences. The cross product of the derivatives yields a vector perpendicular to the surface. When unitized, the vector will have *x* and *y* coordinates in the range -1 to 1. Because a height field cannot overhang itself, the range for *z* is 0 to 1.

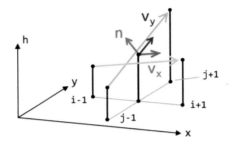

Figure 14-3: Approximating the surface normal at (i, j)

In the following software, *GetNormals* accepts a Targa filename, opens the file, reads a depth map, and then creates an array of unit-length surface normals. Support routines are listed first.

```
float pixelScale = 25;                           // adjust for dif scales
int imgWidth = 0, imgHeight = 0;                 // size of array
char *depthPixels = NULL;                        // ptr to depth array
char *normalPixels = NULL;                       // ptr to normal array

float GetZ(int i, int j) {                       // return depth at (i,j)
    char *v = depthPixels+3*(j*imgWidth+i);      // pixel value 0-255
    return ((float) *v)/255.f;                   // scale to (0,1)
}

float Dz(int i1, int j1, int i2, int j2) {       // z dif bet two pixels
    return GetZ(i2, j2)-GetZ(i1, j1);
}

vec3 Normal(int i, int j) {
    // central differences inside image, forward differences at edge
    int i1 = i > 0? i-1 : i, i2 = i < imgWidth-1? i+1 : i;
    int j1 = j > 0? j-1 : j, j2 = j < imgHeight-1? j+1 : j;
    // approximate partial in x and in y
    vec3 vx((float)(i2-i1)/pixelScale, 0, Dz(i1, j, i2, j));
    vec3 vy(0, (float)(j2-j1)/pixelScale, Dz(i, j1, i, j2));
    vec3 v = cross(vx, vy);
    return normalize(v);                         // v.z should be > 0
}

void GetNormals(const char *depthFilename) {
    // given image file of depth pixels, compute corresponding normals
    // pixelScale compensates for vertical exaggeration
    depthPixels = ReadTarga(depthFilename, imgWidth, imgHeight);
        // read from file, set width, height, return pixels
    int bytesPixel = 3, bytesImage = imgWidth*imgHeight*bytesPixel;
```

```
normalPixels = new char[bytesImage];
char *n = normalPixels;
// store normal as a pixel: 8 bits each for x, y, z (Targa is BGR)
for (int j = 0; j < imgHeight; j++)        // row
    for (int i = 0; i < imgWidth; i++) {   // column
        vec3 v = Normal(i, j);
        *n++ = (char) 127.5f*(v[0]+1);     // [-1,1] maps to red
        *n++ = (char) 127.5f*(v[1]+1);     // [-1,1] maps to green
        *n++ = (char) 255.f*v[2];          // [0,1] maps to blue
    }
}
```

The parameter *pixelScale* compensates for the different scales for the *xy*-plane and for depth. In other words, the ratio between the depth range (nominally 0 to 1) and the image size is fixed at *pixelScale*. (This issue is relevant to the displacement discussed in chapter 19).

In the next figure, at left, concentric waves merge to form a height field; upon processing, the normal map is produced. The *x,y,z* is encoded as *r,g,b*.

As a simple example, we can display a quadrilateral, defined over a texture space of (0,0) to (1,1). When rendering, the pixel shader obtains a surface normal from the normal map. If there is a vertical scale, the inverse scale should be applied to the *z*-coordinate (see section 9.2).

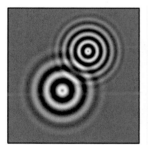 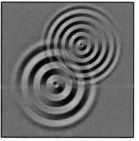 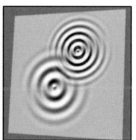

Figure 14-4: Left to right: depth map, normal map, bump-mapped quad

14.2 Local Orientation within a Triangle

Applying bump-mapping to a triangular mesh, rather than a rectangle in the *xy*-plane, requires that the normal obtained from the normal map be transformed by the local surface orientation, that is, a reference frame *UVN* defined by the surface normal and two tangent plane vectors that represent the local *u* and *v* axes. Because the *u* and *v* coordinates at each triangle vertex are arbitrary, the local *u*-axis and *v*-axis are not necessarily perpendicular to each other.

The *u-axis* and *v-axis* can be approximated by forming a correspondence between the 3D gradient of the surface with the 2D gradient of the texture. As *u* and *v* are linearly interpolated across the triangle, the frame *UVN* is constant throughout the triangle.

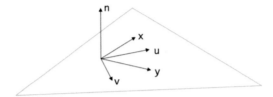

Figure 14-5: Approximating the local *u, v* axes

For example, consider a triangle whose three vertices each consist of a 3D point (x, y, z) and a 2D texture (u, v).

First, we compute the 2D difference in texture and the 3D difference in position along two sides of the triangle:

```
vec3 Dp₁ = p₂-p₁, Dp₂ = p₃-p₁;              // position difs
float du₁ = u₂-u₁, du₂ = u₃-u₁, dv₁ = v₂-v₁, dv₂ = v₃-v₁;  // texture difs
```

We wish to find 3D axes *U* and *V* in the plane of the triangle such that $du_1U+dv_1V = dp_1$ and $du_2U+dv_2V = dp_2$. So,

$$U = (Dp_1 - dv_1V)/du_1 \text{ and } V = (Dp_2 - du_2U)/dv_2$$

Upon substitution:

$$U = (Dp_1 - (dv_1/dv_2)(Dp_2 - du_2U))/du_1 \text{ and } Dp_2 = du_2(Dp_1 - dv_1V)/du_1 + dv_2V$$

yielding the unnormalized, local axes:

(14-1) $U = dv_2Dp_1 - dv_1Dp_2;$
            $V = du_1Dp_2 - du_2Dp_1;$

14.3 Local Orientation at a Vertex

The previous section applies to a single triangle; the reference frame UVN is constant across the triangle. For an arbitrary mesh, the local *UV* coordinate system at a vertex can be set by averaging the *U* and *V* axes computed for each triangle surrounding the vertex. This is calculated by the application, not the GPU.

The *U* and *V* axes are then stored in the vertex buffer; during rendering they are transformed by the vertex shader and interpolated by the rasterizer. At each pixel, the interpolated *U*, *V*, and *N* (normal) vectors produce a local *UVN* coordinate system. Code is given in section 15.6.

As there is now a *UVN* frame per vertex, a frame can be interpolated across a triangle (the special, faceted case where the frame is constant throughout the triangle is presented in sec. 15.3). Thus, with a triangulated mesh, the UVN frame can change throughout the mesh.

14.4 Shader Implementation

Once the bump map has been loaded to the GPU by the application and properly bound in *Display*, it can be used by the pixel shader. To do this, the pixel shader needs the pixel's *uv* coordinates as well as the local *U*-axis and *V*-axis, and surface normal. Thus, the following pixel shader inputs are declared:

```
in vec3 vPoint;
in vec3 vNormal;
in vec2 vUv;
in vec3 vUaxis;
in vec3 vVaxis;
uniform sampler2D bumpMap;
```

First, the shader uses the input *uv* to index a vector from the normal map:

```
vec3 BumpNormal() {
    vec4 bumpV = texture(bumpMap, uv);
    // map red, green to [-1,1], map blue to [0,1]
    vec3 bv = vec3(2*bumpV.r-1, 2*bumpV.g-1, bumpV.b);
    return normalize(bv);
}
```

It is worth noting that GLSL sampler2D values are in a (0,1) range. With OpenGL (see *GetNormals* in 14.1), however, they range 0-255.

124

The bump vector, call it B, can be transformed by the position-less reference frame *UVN* by a matrix operation:

$$B' = MB, \text{ where } M = \begin{bmatrix} U_x & V_x & N_x \\ U_y & V_y & N_y \\ U_z & V_z & N_z \end{bmatrix}$$

The pixel shader can perform this transformation with the following subroutine:

```
vec3 TransformToLocal(vec3 b, vec3 u, vec3 v, vec3 n) {
    // transform vector b by reference frame defined by u, v, n
    float xx = b.x*u.x + b.y*v.x + b.z*n.x;
    float yy = b.x*u.y + b.y*v.y + b.z*n.y;
    float zz = b.x*u.z + b.y*v.z + b.z*n.z;
    return normalize(vec3(xx, yy, zz));
}
```

The main subroutine for the pixel shader can then be given as:

```
void main() {
    vec3 b = BumpNormal();
    vec3 u = normalize(vUaxis), v = normalize(vVaxis),
    vec3 n = TransformToLocal(b, u, v, normalize(N));
    float intensity = PhongIntensity(point, n);
    vec3 color = texture(textureImage, uv).rgb;
    pColor = vec4(intensity*color, 1);
}
```

Although perturbing normals in this way creates the appearance of bumpiness within an object, the silhouette edges of a mesh remain unchanged. We revisit this shortcoming in chapter 20 (tessellation).

14.5 Exercise: Bump-Mapped Triangle

Apply the above section to the exercise from the previous chapter, a texture-mapped triangle, in order to create a bump-mapped triangle. First, find a depth map of interest.

In the next chapter, exercise 15.6, we will apply bump-mapping to an arbitrary mesh.

Chapter 15: Meshes

A collection of triangles and/or quadrilaterals is called a *mesh*. This includes the letter, cube, and face models we've developed in recent chapters. In this chapter we consider their storage and display.

We will use Mesh.h, a library that can read a mesh from a file in one of two popular formats: one (STL) is confined to faceted rendering; the other (OBJ) permits smooth and faceted rendering.

Static vs. Dynamic Arrays

In previous example applications, we've worked with static arrays, such as:

```
float points[][3] = {{x1, y1, z1}, {x2, y2, z2} ...
```

This is an array defined in CPU memory; in this case:

    a) the number of bytes in memory occupied by the array is sizeof(*points*)
    b) the address in memory for the array is given by "points"

For this exercise, however, we use dynamic arrays because the number of vertices and triangles in a file is unknown until it is opened. A simple dynamic array can be declared as follows:

```
std::vector<vec3> points;      // need #include <vector.h>
```

The computation of the array size and address must change:

    a) the number of bytes is points.size()*sizeof(vec3)
    b) the address is &points[0]

15.1 STL File Format: Faceted Rendering

STL is an acronym for Stereo Lithography (also called 3D printing). It is a popular, public format that duplicates all vertices, so that every three points represents a triangle and no vertex is shared between triangles. A surface normal precedes each vertex triplet. Thus, the STL file is readily displayed with *glDrawArrays* and will render as faceted triangles. Each vertex of a triangle has the same normal; there are no other vertex attributes (such as color).

For STL, the 'B' shape (chapter 4) consists of 9 triangles, and, thus, 27 buffered vertices.

An STL file can be ASCII or binary and the subroutine *ReadSTL* (in Mesh.h) parses accordingly. Given a filename, a dynamic array of vertices is filled.

15.2 OBJ File Format: Smooth and Faceted Rendering

OBJ is a more sophisticated format developed by Alias/Wavefront. It supports an arbitrary number of vertices (points), normals, textures (*uv* coordinates) and triangles/polygons. The format supports an arbitrary number of vertices per primitive, but Misc.h divides primitives into triangles. Colors per vertex are not supported.

The cube, face, and VW beetle underscore the need to accommodate faceted surfaces as well as smooth surfaces with possible creases. In chapter 9, we achieved faceted shading by duplicating vertices (same location, different surface normals). The OBJ format permits surfaces that are smooth, faceted, or smooth with creases by selectively duplicating vertices when necessary.

The binary file format for OBJ is proprietary; the ASCII format is public and is implemented in Mesh.cpp by *ReadOBJ*.

Central to the OBJ format is the specification of a vertex as a triplet of indices: an index into a point location array, an index into a surface normal array, and an index into a *uv*-coordinate array.

Two vertices are identical if their triplet identifiers are equal. Thus, if adjacent triangles whose shared vertices have the same triplet identifier, the edge between them will be smooth; otherwise, it will be creased (meaning discontinuous in texture, surface normal, or both).

Thus, points, normals, and textures can be defined without a one-to-one correspondence. For example, the 'B' is flat, so only one normal need be stored in the file and all the vertices would have the same normal index (i.e., 0).

A typical triangle specification consists of three triplets: each triplet contains the indices for point, normal, and texture for one of the triangle vertices. Vertices with the same three indices are identical and need be buffered only once.

ReadOBJ uses the standard template library *map* class to build the vertex array and triangle indices. From the OBJ triangle specifications, a set of unique vertices is createed, indexed by an integer triangle array suitable for *glDrawElements*.

15.3 Faceted vs. Smooth (an epilogue)

Let us consider this issue one last time. Suppose we have a smooth mesh, in which vertices are shared, that we wish to display in a faceted manner. It would appear from our prior discussions that this would require an expanded GPU vertex buffer, one in which vertices are duplicated. An expanded vertex buffer is reasonable for some situations, but it is unneeded if the entire mesh is to be facet-shaded.

When OpenGL processes vertex data through the rasterizer, it does so in parallel, with a minimum of four pixels in a square block being shaded at the same time. Thus, the rasterizer is able to calculate the change in any vertex attribute at any pixel. OpenGL provides functions *dFdx* and *dFdy* that can be used to calculate the surface normal as follows:

```
vec3 dx = dFdy(gPosition.xyz);   // constant over entire triangle
vec3 dy = dFdx(gPosition.xyz);   // ditto
vec3 n = normalize(cross(dx, dy));
```

Thus, a faceted appearance can be achieved without buffering surface normals.

A Faceted, Local UVN Frame

The *dFdx* and *dFdy* functions described above can determine the local change of any quantity that is interpolated by the rasterizer. This allows us to simplify a result from the previous chapter (bump-mapping).

Section 14.2 presented the calculation of local *U* and *V* axes that can be stored in a vertex buffer and, after rasterization, passed to the pixel shader. This allows the local *UVN* frame to be interpolated from vertex to vertex across a triangle. If a faceted appearance is desired, however, the computation, storage, and movement through the pipeline of the *U* and *V* axes can be replaced with code in the pixel shader. The GPU can compute the reference frame for each pixel and produce the transformed, bump-mapped normal with the following.

```
vec2 du = dFdy(teUv), dv = dFdx(teUv);
vec3 dx = dFdy(tePoint), dy = dFdx(tePoint);
vec3 U = normalize(du.x*dx+du.y*dy);
vec3 V = normalize(dv.x*dx+dv.y*dy);
vec3 N = normalize(teNormal);
vec3 B = BumpNormal();           // see sec. 14.4
vec3 XN = TransformToLocal(B, U, V, N);
vec3 n = normalize(XN);
```

15.4 Back-face Culling

The *Euler Characteristic*, another contribution from Leonhard Euler, is relevant to meshes. It is the relationship

$V-E+F = 2-2G,$

where V is the number of vertices, F is the number of faces, E is the number of edges, and G is the genus of a 3D mesh. With an OBJ file, the number of edges is easily counted, but this is not so with an STL file.

Genus can be understood as the number of holes through an object, 0 for a sphere, 1 for a torus, etc.

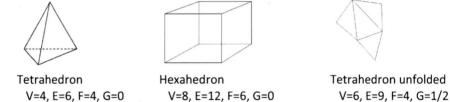

Tetrahedron	Hexahedron	Tetrahedron unfolded
V=4, E=6, F=4, G=0	V=8, E=12, F=6, G=0	V=6, E=9, F=4, G=1/2

Figure 15-1: Examples of the Euler Characteristic

The Euler characteristic tells us whether we have a closed (or *manifold*) mesh, i.e., one in which all edges are shared by two and only two primitives. If so, and assuming surface normals point outwards, then any primitive whose face normal points away from the camera will be covered by forward-facing primitives. So, rendering performance can be increased simply by culling those back-facing primitives:

```
glFrontFace(GL_CCW);        // front-face should be ccw
glEnable(GL_CULL_FACE);     // don't display back faces
```

For meshes that are not closed, however, an interesting problem arises and is discussed in sec. 20-7.

15.5 Exercise: Texture-mapped Mesh

In this exercise we will map texture onto a mesh. The texture will be in the form of an image file, and the mesh can be either the face from Exercise 10.2 or a mesh downloaded from the web.

STEP I: Obtain a 3D mesh with *uv*-coordinates

If using Face

> Use your application from Exercise 10-2 (Phong-Shaded Face) in which your mesh data is 'hard-wired' in the application (i.e., not in a file).

If using OBJ File

> Download one of the many "OBJ" files freely available online; it must contain *point*, *normal*, and *texture* vertex data (many do, many don't).

> Add Mesh.h and Mesh.cpp to your project.

> Download Stub-ShadeMeshOBJ.cpp to serve as the template for your application. Test that it produces a Phong-shaded image.

STEP 2: Make a Targa image file

Now, download/copy an image you like, or, for those working with a face, use the unpainted face image.

Convert the image to .tga (Targa) format, if necessary (this is easily done with a program like *IrfanView*, freely available online). ***Be sure the resulting file is 24bpp.*** In order to read the file, add Misc.h and Misc.cpp to your project.

STEP 3: Modify the application

3A) Add an array for texture coordinates

In addition to the points and normals that should already be defined in your application, add an array for the texture coordinates:

```
vector<vec2> uvs;                          // vertex texture coordinates
```

If using Face

Set the *uvs* array to be the same as the (*x*, *y*) coordinates of the face vertices.

If using OBJ File

Add "&uvs" as the last argument to the call to *ReadAsciiObj* (in *main*).

In *InitVertexBuffer*, the vertex buffer must be enlarged to accommodate the *uv* coordinates, and the *uv* data should be copied using *glBufferSubData*.

3B) Initialize the Texture Image

Instructions to load texture are given in exercise 12.4.

3C) Changes to the Vertex Shader

The vertex shader needs an additional input and output for texture coordinates:

```
in vec2 uv;
out ve2 vuv;
```

In exercise 12.4, the *uv* was copied unchanged to *vuv*. For the present exercise, in order to facilitate alignment of the texture with the mesh, we'll provide a general transformation capability via an input texture matrix:

```
uniform mat4 textureTransform = mat4(1);
```

textureTransform defaults to an identity matrix, meaning it will not affect the texture coordinates unless specifically modified by the application. The vertex shader can output the transformed *uv* as follows:

```
vuv = (textureTransform*vec4(uv, 0, 1)).xy;
```

A texture transformation can be created and downloaded in *Display*:

```
float dx = 0, dy = 0, s = 1;
```

```
mat4 t = Translate(dx, dy, 0)*Scale(s);
SetUniform(program, "textureTransform", t);
```

The default values for *dx*, *dy* and *s* can be adjusted to size and position the texture on the mesh. This can be especially useful in aligning the face texture with the face mesh.

3D) Changes to the Pixel Shader

The pixel shader needs an additional input:

> in vec2 vuv;

To gain access to the texture map stored in GPU memory, the pixel shader accepts a uniform "sampler2D" identifier:

```
uniform sampler2D textureImage;
```

A pixel value is then accessed by a call to the GLSL function *texture*, providing the *uv-*coordinates sent from the rasterizer:

```
vec3 color = texture(textureImage, vuv).rgb;
```

This color, modified by the shading intensity, is then output by the pixel shader.

If all goes well, you'll be rewarded with your own, personal avatar.

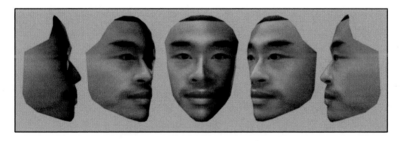

Figure 15-2: Texture-mapped mesh
(courtesy Chun-Chi Huang and Siyao Xu)

15.6 Exercise: Bump-Mapped Mesh

We can begin this exercise with code from the prior assignment (texture-mapped mesh), or with Stub-ShadeMeshOBJ.cpp. We should have an array of vertex locations and corresponding surface normals and *uv*-coordinates, and vertex connectivity defined by a triangles array:

```
vector<vec3> points;
vector<vec3> normals;
vector<vec2> textures;
vector<int3> triangles;
```

Test that you are able to produce a Phong-shaded image of the mesh.

Create the U and V Axes

To implement bump-mapping, we need to apply equation 14.1 to each triangle, and average the result at each vertex, per section 14.2. First, the *u* and *v* axes are declared:

```
vector<vec3> us, vs; // u axes and v axes, per vertex
```

The following routine iterates through the triangles, accumulating the *U* and *V* axes at the triangle vertices, and then normalize the results:

```
void SetAxes() {
    us.resize(points.size());
    vs.resize(points.size());
    for (size_t i = 0; i < triangles.size(); i++) {
        int3 t = triangles[i];
        vec3 p1 = points[t.i1], p2 = points[t.i2], p3 = points[t.i3];
        vec2 t1=textures[t.i1], t2=textures[t.i2], t3=textures[t.i3];
        vec3 dp1 = p2-p1, dp2 = p3-p1;        // position differences
        vec2 dt1 = t2-t1, dt2 = t3-t1;        // texture differences
        vec3 uAxis = dt2[1]*dp1-dt1[1]*dp2;   // compute local u axis
        vec3 vAxis = dt1[0]*dp2-dt2[0]*dp1;   // local v axis
        // accumulate triangle u,v axis at each vertex
        us[t.i1] += uAxis; us[t.i2] += uAxis; us[t.i3] += uAxis;
        vs[t.i1] += vAxis; vs[t.i2] += vAxis; vs[t.i3] += vAxis;
    }
    // unitize the axes
    for (size_t i = 0; i < points.size(); i++) {
        us[i] = normalize(us[i]);
        vs[i] = normalize(vs[i]);
    }
}
```

The vertex buffer must allocate additional memory for the *u* and *v* axes:

```
int nVrts = points.size();
int sizeVrt = 4*sizeof(vec3)+sizeof(vec2);
  // uaxis, vaxis, point, normal, u, v
```

```
glBufferData(GL_ARRAY_BUFFER, nVrts*sizeVrt, NULL, GL_STATIC_DRAW);
```

And the *u* and *v* axes can be stored after the points, normals, and textures:

```
int sizePts = nVrts*sizeof(vec3), sizeTex = nVrts*sizeof(vec2);
glBufferSubData(GL_ARRAY_BUFFER, 2*sizePts+sizeTex, sizePts, &us[0]);
glBufferSubData(GL_ARRAY_BUFFER, 3*sizePts+sizeTex, sizePts, &vs[0]);
```

Create Texture and Normal Maps

As described in the textured triangle exercise (section 12.4), a texture map requires an OpenGL *texture name* and *texture unit*. In this exercise we use two maps: one for texture (colors) and one for normals (bumps). The following variables control the two maps:

```
GLuint textureName, normalName;
int textureUnit = 0, normalUnit = 1;
```

If the texture and bump maps are from files, then the OpenGL 'names' are set:

```
// read texture and bump images from file, store in GPU
textureName = LoadTexture(textureFilename, textureUnit);
normalName = LoadTexture(normalFilename, normalUnit);
```

(Here, 'texture' is used in two ways: a generic reference to any 2D image and, specifically, a map for coloring.)

If only a depth file is available, the bump map can be computed if the application calls the *GetNormals* subroutine given in section 14.1 (found in Misc.h). *GetNormals* returns *normalPixels*, which can be deleted after the call to *LoadTexture*:

```
normalName = LoadTexture(normalPixels, normalUnit);
delete [] normalPixels;
```

Normal maps are widely available on the web; depth maps are not as common. Paired bump and texture maps or paired depth and texture maps are hard to find, but can yield convincing images.

Changes to Shaders

The vertex shader will be fed a *u*-axis and *v*-axis for each vertex, so these need to be declared as inputs and outputs:

```
in vec3 uAxis;
in vec3 vAxis;
out vec3 vUaxis;
out vec3 vVaxis;
```

and the vectors must be transformed by the view:

```
vUaxis = (modelview*vec4(uaxis, 0)).xyz;
vVaxis = (modelview*vec4(vaxis, 0)).xyz;
```

The pixel shader must declare input *u* and *v* axes:

```
in vec3 vUaxis;
in vec3 vVaxis;
```

and input uniforms for the maps:

```
uniform sampler2D textureMap;
uniform sampler2D normalMap;
```

The procedures *BumpNormal* and *TransformToLocal*, given in section 14.4, must be included with the pixel shader. The *main* routine looks like:

```
void main() {
    vec3 n = BumpNormal();
    vec3 nn = TransformToLocal(n, vUaxis, vVaxis, vNormal);
    float intensity = PhongIntensity(vPoint, nn);
    vec3 color = texture(textureMap, vUv).rgb;
    pColor = vec4(intensity*color, 1);
}
```

Changes to Display

The unit identifier is used in setting the active texture and the pixel shader sampler2D uniform; the name identifier is used to bind the active texture. Thus, in *Display*, the appropriate textures are activated and uniforms are set as follows:

```
glActiveTexture(GL_TEXTURE0+textureUnit);
glBindTexture(GL_TEXTURE_2D, textureName);
SetUniform(shaderId, "textureMap", textureUnit);
glActiveTexture(GL_TEXTURE0+normalUnit);
glBindTexture(GL_TEXTURE_2D, normalName);
SetUniform(shaderId, "normalMap", normalUnit);
```

Two additional vertex attribute pointers must be established for the *u* and *v* axes:

```
int nPts = points.size();
int sizePts = nPts*sizeof(vec3), sizeTex = nPts*sizeof(vec2);
VertexAttribPointer(programId, "uaxis", 3, 0,
                    (void *) (2*sizePts+sizeTex));
VertexAttribPointer(programId, "vaxis", 3, 0,
                    (void *) (3*sizePts+sizeTex));
```

The following example was generated with these techniques.

Figure 15-3: texture and normal maps; bump-mapped teacup
(depth and texture data courtesy Gene Cooper)

The sense of depth is improved by a moving light source. In the following image, the light source is shown as a red dot; as it is moved, the bas-relief becomes apparent.

Figure 15-4: Close-ups, different lights

15.7 Exercise: Multiple Meshes

With this exercise, we wish to read and display multiple meshes within a single application. This task is made easier with a class:

```
class Mesh {
public:
    Mesh();
    int id;
    string filename;
    vector<int3> triangles;
    mat4 xform;          // object to world space
    GLuint vBufferId;    // bind for display
    void InitBuffer(char *fullpath, int id) {
        vector<vec3> points;
        vector<vec3> normals;
        vector<vec2> uvs;
        if (!ReadAsciiObj(fullpath, points, triangles, &normals, &uvs)) {
            printf("can't read %s\n", filename);
            return;
        }
        < set vBufferId, filename, id >
        < fill GPU vertex buffer >
    }
    void Draw();
};
```

The application should support some simple interaction, such as selection of a mesh and movement of the mesh using the Mover class (see chapter 11).

A more sophisticated application could include keyboard commands to read a new mesh, read a different texture, delete a mesh, list all the meshes in a scene, save a scene, and read a scene.

Chapter 16: Parametric Curves

In the 1960s, Pierre Bézier (Bay-Zee-Ay) oversaw an effort at Renault Car Company to design and manufacture automobiles numerically. He developed the polynomial curve and surface that bear his name. The curve would prove useful in fields related to computer graphics, including geometric design, manufacturing, and typography.

In 1998, Bézier reflected:

> *Modification of a curve was accomplished … by distorting the Cartesian cube in which it was … defined. For the sake of simplicity, the distortion … would be linear, or affine. Hence the cube would become a parallelepiped … distorting a pppd only requires moving four points; … it seemed simple – how simple! – to put those vectors end to end, thus building an open polygon the shape of which mimics that of the corresponding curve.*

Figure 16-1: Pierre Bézier

The 'open polygon' is called the *control polygon*.

16.1 De Casteljau Construction and the Bézier Curve

Paul de Casteljau invented the same curve predating Bézier, but did not publish until later. He developed a geometric construction using linear interpolation, recursively applied to the edges of the control polygon in order to compute a point on the curve at parametric location *t* (where *t* ranges 0 through 1).

138

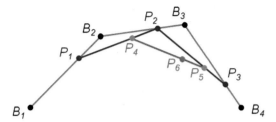

Figure 16-2: The de Casteljau construction

Polynomial Form

To express this algebraically, given the *control points* B_1, B_2, B_3, and B_4, we first compute three interpolated points along the three control segments:

$P_1 = B_1+t(B_2-B_1)$; $P_2 = B_2+t(B_3-B_2)$; $P_3 = B_3+t(B_4-B_3)$

Then, we compute two points along the two segments defined by P_1, P_2, and P_3:

$P_4 = P_1+t(P_2-P_1)$; $P_5 = P_2+t(P_3-P_2)$

From these two points a final point on the curve is computed:

$P_6 = P_4+t(P_5-P_4)$

If the above arithmetic is expanded and regrouped:

(16-1) $P(t) = (-t^3+3t^2-3t+1)B_1+(3t^3-6t^2+3t)B_2+(-3t^3+3t^2)B_3+t^3B_4$

The polynomial functions weighting the B_i are cubic, and so the Bézier curve is a *cubic polynomial curve* defined by four control points. It interpolates its outer two control points, and approximates its inner two control points. (The *quadratic* Bézier curve is defined by three points, but the cubic is generally preferred for its greater flexibility.)

Matrix Form

Equation (16-1) can be represented in matrix form:

$$P(t) = \begin{bmatrix} -t^3 & 3t^3 & -3t^3 & t^3 \\ 3t^2 & -6t^2 & 3t^2 & 0 \\ -3t & 3t & 0 & 0 \\ 1 & 0 & 0 & 0 \end{bmatrix} \begin{bmatrix} B_1 \\ B_2 \\ B_3 \\ B_4 \end{bmatrix}$$

139

$$= [t^3 \ t^2 \ t \ 1] \begin{bmatrix} -1 & 3 & -3 & 1 \\ 3 & -6 & 3 & 0 \\ -3 & 3 & 0 & 0 \\ 1 & 0 & 0 & 0 \end{bmatrix} \begin{bmatrix} B_1 \\ B_2 \\ B_3 \\ B_4 \end{bmatrix}$$

$$= [t^3 \ t^2 \ t \ 1] \ [M] \begin{bmatrix} B_1 \\ B_2 \\ B_3 \\ B_4 \end{bmatrix} = [t^3 \ t^2 \ t \ 1] \begin{bmatrix} C_1 \\ C_2 \\ C_3 \\ C_4 \end{bmatrix}$$

where the B_i are the three-dimensional control points and C_i are the three-dimensional polynomial coefficients for the curve. Thus, we can evaluate the Bézier curve directly from the control points and M, or, more efficiently, with the coefficients, C.

Basis Functions

The four polynomial functions weighting the four control points, B_1 through B_4, are called *basis functions* and they belong to the family of *Bernstein polynomials*.

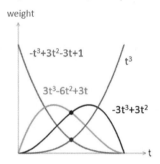

weight

$-t^3+3t^2-3t+1$

t^3

$3t^3-6t^2+3t$

$-3t^3+3t^2$

t

Figure 16-3: Bernstein basis functions for Bézier curve

16.2 Derivatives

As the polynomials are degree three, the curve has continuous first and second derivatives. Differentiating with respect to t, dP/dt yields the *velocity* (i.e., *tangent*) of the curve:

$V(t) = (-3t^2+6t-3)B_1+(9t^2-12t+3)B_2+(-9t^2+6t)B_3+3t^2B_4$

Differentiating once more yields the *acceleration* of the curve:

$A(t) = (-6t+6)B_1+(18t-12)B_2+(-18t+6)B_3+6tB_4$

140

Curvature → 密切图

For a given point on the curve, the *curvature* points towards the center of the "osculating circle". Its *magnitude* is given by $K = 1/r$, where is r is the radius of the circle. The smaller the radius, the higher the curvature.

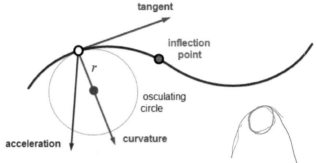

Figure 16-4: Features of a curve

The curvature vector can be computed by:

vec3 N = cross(velocity, acceleration); // normal to plane of circle
vec3 K = normalize(cross(N, tangent)); // unit-length curvature vector

The cubic Bézier curve, being degree three, can contain an *inflection point*. This is a point where curvature is zero (and the curvature vector is undefined); it occurs if acceleration is zero or parallel with the tangent.

16.3 Reference Frame on the Curve

关 数矩阵.

A reference frame can be computed directly from a parametric curve. Given a parametric location t, the point p is given by a cubic polynomial, from which v (velocity) is the derivative and n (the normal) is $v \times a$ where a is the acceleration, and b (the 'bi-normal') is $v \times n$. The v, n, and b form the reference frame.

$$\begin{bmatrix} n_x & b_x & v_x & p_x \\ n_y & b_y & v_y & p_x \\ n_z & b_z & v_z & p_x \\ 0 & 0 & 0 & 1 \end{bmatrix}$$

141

This matrix will transform the origin to p, the x-axis to n, the y-axis to b, and the z-axis to v.

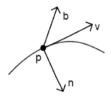

Figure 16-5: The Frenet frame

16.4 Properties

Not Arc-length Parameterized

In figure 16-4, acceleration is not perpendicular to the curve. This is because a cubic polynomial curve is *not arc-length parameterized*, that is, a change in t does not produce a proportional change in distance traveled along the curve.

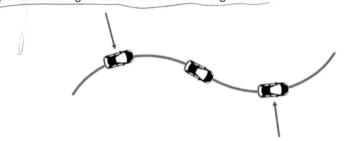

Figure 16-6: Force along a curve

The movement of a car traveling at a constant speed, however, is arc-length parameterized. Passengers experience the force of acceleration along the curve perpendicular to the direction of travel: in making a right turn, a passenger is pushed from the left; in making a left turn, the push is from the right. At the inflection point, there is no push.

Subdivision

Subdivision of a curve into two pieces is equivalent to points generated by the de Casteljau construction; in the illustration below, for $t = \frac{1}{2}$, B_1-B_4 are replaced with L_1-L_4 and R_1-R_4.

142

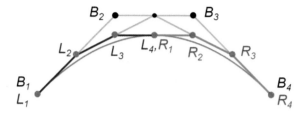

Figure 16-7: Subdivision of a curve into left and right pieces

Convex Hull Property

The entire curve is contained within the *convex hull* of the control points (i.e., the polygon formed by connecting B_1 through B_4 and back to B_1. This permits the use of several algorithms related to hit-testing, clipping and rendering.

16.5 The Hermite Curve

Tangents at the ends of the Bézier curve are:

$V_0 = 3(B_2-B_1)$
$V_1 = 3(B_4-B_3)$

A Bézier curve may be defined in *Hermite form*, which is the two endpoints and the two end tangents, i.e., B_1, B_4, V_0, and V_1. The two forms are closely related.

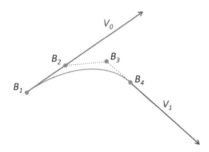

Figure 16-8: Bézier and Hermite representations

16.6 Piecewise Continuous Curves

A piecewise Bézier curve consists of two or more sets of control polygons. If the last point of one set is the same as the first point of the next set, the curves will have positional continuity (C^0 *continuity*). For tangent (C^1) continuity, the last segment of one

143

set must be colinear with the first segment of the next set. And if those two segments are the same length (in the figure below, $|B_3B_4|$ = $|B_4B_5|$), then the curves meet with curvature (C^2) continuity.

More sophisticated methods can minimize torsion and/or maintain curvature along piecewise curves (see, e.g., *Mathematical Elements for Computer Graphics* by Rogers).

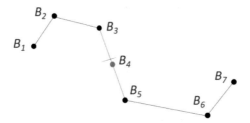

Figure 16-9: Two Bézier curves and their control polygons

16.7 Rendering Bézier Curves

A Bézier curve is usually rendered *piecewise-linearly*, i.e., the curve is broken into *res* number of straight segments. The curve defined by control points B_1 through B_4 can be rendered in this way with the code below. It's assumed a function *BezierPoint* has been defined to compute position, and that the GPU buffers referenced by *glBindBuffer* have been generated.

```
glBindBuffer(GL_ARRAY_BUFFER, lineBuffer);
VertexAttribPointer(shader, "point", 3, 0,(void*) 0);
vec3 pts[] = {b[0], b[0]};
for (int k = 1; k <= res; k++) {
    pts[1] = BezierPoint((float) k/res, b[0], b[1], b[2], b[3]);
    glBufferData(GL_ARRAY_BUFFER,2*sizeof(vec3),pts,GL_STATIC_DRAW);
    glDrawArrays(GL_LINES, 0, 2);
    pts[0] = pts[1];
}
```

The need to send buffer data from the CPU to the GPU at every iteration slows the execution. This can be remedied by sending all the vertex data at once, and then connecting the vertices via the GL primitive LINE_STRIP:

```
std::vector<vec3> points(res+1);
int sizePts = (res+1)*sizeof(vec3);
glBindBuffer(GL_ARRAY_BUFFER, lineStripBuffer);
```

144

```
VertexAttribPointer(shader, "point", 3, 0, (void *) 0);
for (int k = 0; k <= res; k++)
    points[k] = BezierPoint((float) k/res, b[0], b[1], b[2], b[3]);
glBufferData(GL_ARRAY_BUFFER, sizePts, &points[0], GL_STATIC_DRAW);
glDrawArrays(GL_LINE_STRIP, 0, res+1);
```

In chapter 20 we will introduce the tessellation shader. We'll see that it offers an additional way to render a curve.

16.8 Exercise: *et Maintenant*, Bézier!

With this exercise we create a program such that the user can directly manipulate control points, creating a 3D Bézier curve.

The stub application 16-StubBezierCurve.cpp contains a Bézier class whose subroutine templates are defined, but not the bodies – that's the exercise. Also, initial locations for the four control points must be specified.

The *BezierPoint* subroutine should implement the polynomial form given in equation (16-1).

The application does not define any shaders because it does its drawing via Draw.h, which defines its own, relatively simple, shader program. Use subroutine *Line* to connect two points and use *Disk* to round an endpoint; before these calls, *UseDrawShader* must be called.

The stub application contains mouse callbacks that support user selection and movement of a Bézier control point, but the body for Bezier::PickPoint must be completed.

△

Bonuses

1. Animate a dot on the curve, moving from one end to the other, back and forth.

Hints: display the point after the curve and its control mesh are drawn. Send *Disk* a point computed on the curve whose *t*-parameter varies according to time (disabling the *z*-buffer might be a good idea). We did something similar in exercise 5.3, computing $sin(dt)$ as an animation parameter, which requires defining the application's start time.

2. Create two curves, not one, such that the last point of the first control mesh is the same as the first point of the second control mesh. Maintain C^2 continuity (that is, continuity of tangent and curvature) by ensuring that the 3rd, 4th, and 5th control points are collinear, and that the 4th point is midway between the 3rd and 5th, such as in figure 16-9.

Chapter 17: Text

Bézier developed his curve to improve automotive design and manufacture, but it has become widespread in the design of digital fonts. Beginning in the early nineteen-seventies, Peter Karow augmented straight lines and circular arcs with quadratic Bézier curves to define the outlines of font characters.

Because outline (or *vector*) fonts are defined by analytic equations, arbitrary scaling does not affect their precision (unlike the more primitive 'bitmap fonts' that are defined by an array of pixels).

In the late 1970s, John Warnock joined an effort at Xerox PARC to develop a *device-independent page description language*, utilizing cubic Bézier curves. This evolved into the Turing-complete PostScript language, developed by Warnock at Adobe.

Figure 17-1: John Warnock
(used with permission)

In this photograph Dr. Warnock illustrates the use of outlines. The de Casteljau construction is visible in the upper left, and the character 'a' is sectioned into piecewise Bézier curves.

Although computer fonts are ubiquitous in text editing, formatting, and printing, they receive little support from graphics APIs or toolkits. Neither OpenGL nor GLFW provide text support.

Quality font display is not too difficult given modern shader architecture, freely available typefaces, and a freely available typeface library. In this chapter we develop software to render text on a screen at any size or orientation, with selectable font faces.

17.1 Displaying Text

Numerous techniques to display anti-aliased text have been described over the decades.

With the advent of high-speed processing and large memory, a modern solution is to pre-compute high-resolution shaded images (*opacity maps*) of individual characters (and pieces of characters, called 'glyphs') within a font. These images can be scaled to various font sizes and positioned according to metrics associated with the font.

17-Demo-FontTest.cpp is our example program to display text. It depends on three components:

a file defining font outlines,
a routine to read the file and rasterize the font characters, and
OpenGL code to display each character.

We will use the TrueType file format and the FreeType font library.

TrueType (a file format)

TrueType is a file format that defines a given (named) typeface. It consists of a *character set*, which is a collection of glyph outline curves. Many conventional and custom TrueType typefaces are online and free to download.

FreeType (a font library)

The FreeType library provides a function to read typeface files of several formats, although our examples will use TrueType. We use FreeType to prepare an opacity map for each typeface glyph; these maps can be created at arbitrary resolution.

17.2 The Text Library

Text.h provides for the construction of a character set (see *SetCharacterSet*) and then displayscharacter strings (see *Text*). These routines are simple to call; in this section, we review their inner workings.

The subroutine *SetCharacterSet* initializes FreeType and reads the named typeface from a file:

```
#include "Text.h"
```

```
FT_Library ft;
FT_Face face;
FT_Init_FreeType(&ft);
FT_New_Face(ft, typefaceFilename, 0, &face);
```

The glyph metrics are then read for each printable character. These control the positioning of each character with respect to the previous character, thus allowing *variable pitch* (i.e., different letters require different amounts of space; this is not the same as *kerning*).

The glyph's curve descriptions are read and an opacity map is rendered. From *SetCharacterSet*:

```
FT_Load_Char(face, c, FT_LOAD_RENDER);
glTexImage2D(..., face->glyph->bitmap.buffer);
```

The texture indices, glyph metrics, and opacity maps are stored in a *Character* class, defined in Text.h. An array of all printable characters forms the *character set*.

Rendering

Once a character set is initialized, a string may be displayed beginning at pixel (xp, yp), with a given scale, by the loop below (from *RenderText* in Text.cpp). First, the view transformation must be set to screen space:

```
UseDrawShader(ScreenMode());

for (const char *c = text; *c; c++) {      // loop thru chars in text
    Character ch = characters[(int)*c];   // obtain ch from set
    float x = xp+ch.bearing.i1*scale; );  // set render location, size
    float y = yp-(ch.gSize.i2-ch.bearing.i2)*scale;
    float w = ch.gSize.i1*scale, h = ch.gSize.i2*scale;
    glBindTexture(GL_TEXTURE_2D, ch.textureID); // enable ch texture
    // update vertex memory; each vertex: x,y,u,v
    float quad[][4]={{x,y+h,0,0},{x+w,y+h,1,0},{x+w,y,1,1},{x,y,0,1}};
    glBufferSubData(GL_ARRAY_BUFFER, 0, sizeof(quad), quad);
    glDrawArrays(GL_QUADS, 0, 4);          // render glyph texture with quad
    xp += (ch.advance >> 6)*scale;         // adv. char. posn wrt 1/64 pixel
}
```

The first vertex of the quadrilateral is at pixel location (xp, yp) offset by the glyph's "bearing". The other three vertices complete the definition of a quadrilateral of width w and height h.

149

The vertices are copied to a GPU buffer, and then drawn by a call to *glDrawArrays*. The quadrilateral can be rendered with any given color; the opacity varies according to the glyph's opacity map.

The location of the four vertices is augmented with (u,v) texture coordinates. Within the quadrilateral, the rasterizer will interpolate the geometric location and the *uv* coordinates of a pixel. The pixel shader then determines a pixel's opacity given the interpolated *uv* coordinates and the specified uniform sampler2D "glyphImage":

```
pColor = vec4(color, texture(glyphImage, uv).r);
```

17.3 Arbitrary Text Orientation

The quadrilateral's vertices are 2D and are perhaps best thought of as defined in "text space". As we display each character, the quadrilateral moves parallel to the screen's positive *x*-axis. There are two routines in Text.cpp that position text parallel to the screen: one positions the text in pixel coordinates, the other positions the text at a 3D location transformed to the screen.

A character can be arbitrarily oriented, however, if the vertices of the quadrilateral are transformed.

For example, suppose we'd like a spiral of text. Rather than move the quadrilateral along the *x*-axis, we could move it along a spiral path. Referring to the subroutine *RenderText* in Text.cpp, we can produce a spiral if we replace this declaration:

```
float quad[][4] = {{x,y+h,0,0},{x+w,y+h,1,0},{x+w,y,1,1},{x,y,0,1}};
```

with the following:

```
vec2 Spiral(float t) {
    float alpha = t/50, mag = .3f*alpha*alpha;
    return mag*vec2(cos(alpha), sin(alpha));
}
vec2 c(winWidth/2, winHeight/2);     // center of screen
vec2 p1 = Spiral(x), p2 = Spiral(x+w), p3 = 1.2f*p2, p4 = 1.2f*p1;
vec4 quad[] = {vec4(c+p1,0,0), vec4(c+p2,1,0),
               vec4(c+p3,1,1), vec4(c+p4,0,1)};
```

This transforms all points by the spiral pattern, which not only changes position, but scale and orientation as well:

Figure 17-2: Spiraled text

17.4 Exercise

Part 1: Test FreeType

From the online exercises, follow FreetypeSetup.doc. It may not be possible to satisfy the linker; in which case these exercises cannot be completed.

Assuming the linker is happy, download a font from a website offering free FreeType typefaces; modify 17-Demo-FontTest.cpp to display at least one line of text with this new font (the message and font should be different from the original examples).

Part 2: Flexed Text

FontTest and the spiral example display text parallel with the screen. But the quadrilateral that displays a glyph can be of any orientation. The RenderText function in Text.cpp allows any string to be transformed by a 4 X 4 matrix.

So, for this exercise, we'll modify the Bézier curve exercise from chapter 16 so that text, character by character, is positioned along a Bézier curve. The result should look like:

Figure 17-3: Text oriented by a Bézier curve

The *Bezier* class from the previous chapter must be augmented with a method to define a reference frame, described in section 16.3. The exercise requires us to complete the following subroutines:

```
Velocity(float t) { ... }
Acceleration(float t) { ... }
Curvature(float t) { ... }
```

Calculation of the reference frame is given below. (Unlike the *n, b, v* frame, this is *v, n, b*, meaning the *x*-axis is transformed to be tangent with the curve, the *y*-axis is transformed to align with the curve's curvature, and the *z*-axis is perpendicular to the plane of curvature. Thus, the characters should be readable along the curve, not edgewise to the curve.

```
mat4 Frame(float t) {
    vec3 p = Point(t), v = Velocity(t), n = normalize(Curvature(t));
    vec3 b = normalize(cross(v, n));
    mat4 m;                             // defaults to identity
    for (int i = 0; i < 3; i++) {       // set reference frame
        m[i][0] = v[i];
        m[i][1] = n[i];
        m[i][2] = b[i];
        m[i][3] = p[i];
    }
    return m;
}
```

The task now is to display a text string character by character, following along the curve. We can display char *c* at parametric position *t* with the following:

```
const char buf[] = {c, 0};  // single char and null terminator
mat4 f = curve.Frame(t);
RenderText(buf, 0, 0, vec3(0,0,0), 10, camera.fullview*f);
```

The transformation matrix sent to *RenderText* is the camera view (i.e., *persp**modelview) multiplied by the curve's reference frame *f* at location *t*.

Bonus

What happens if the curve inflects? How might this be remedied?

Chapter 18: Parametric Patches

18.1 The Coons Patch

In 1967, Steven Coons published his famed "little red book", which introduced a new mathematical representation and geometric interpretation for a surface as a set of adjacent 'patches'. The basic concepts are in wide use today. Coons served on Ivan Sutherland's doctoral committee, and in his name SIGGRAPH bestows its biennial lifetime achievement award.

Figure 18-1: Steven Coons

The classic Coons patch is defined over a square domain by four, connected boundary curves (in the figure below, C_1-C_4). It is the sum of three *ruled surfaces*, namely: two surfaces defined by straight lines connecting opposite boundaries, minus the surface defined by connecting opposite edges of the quadrilateral formed by the corners. The first two linearly interpolate between two curves, the third is a bilinear interpolation.

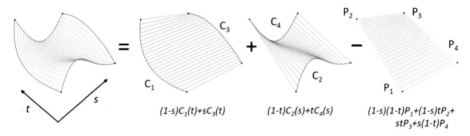

$$(1-s)C_1(t)+sC_3(t) \qquad (1-t)C_2(s)+tC_4(s) \qquad \begin{array}{l}(1-s)(1-t)P_1+(1-s)tP_2+\\stP_3+s(1-t)P_4\end{array}$$

Figure 18-2: Formulation of a Coons patch

The patch interpolates the four defining boundary curves. These are often cubic polynomials (like the Bézier) due to their design flexibility; this implies four control points per side, with the corners shared, for a total of 12 control points.

153

Adjacent patches are coincident along their shared boundary, but tangent continuity (C^1) and curvature continuity (C^2) are difficult to establish. They are more readily established with *Bézier patches*.

18.2 The Bézier Patch

The (cubic) Bézier patch uses the same 12 control points as a Coons patch to establish the patch boundaries, and adds four control points internal to the patch.

These 16 control points may be treated as control points for four Bézier curves in the *s*-direction or four Bezier curves in the *t*-direction. For example, in the illustration below, the control points are grouped four at a time to define four red curves.

Using either method from sec. 16-1, these four *s*-curves can each be evaluated at parametric value *s*, resulting in four red points. These four points define the blue curve, which, when evaluated at *t*, produces *P(s, t)*, a point on the patch. An evaluation in the *t*-direction first and then in the *s*-direction yields the same result.

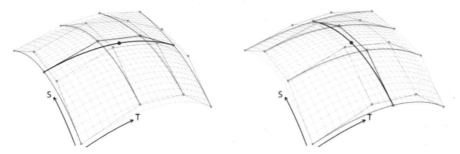

Figure 18-3: Bézier patch evaluation

Each point on the surface is a product of two cubic polynomials; the first weights the control points in the *s* parametric direction; the second in the *t* direction. This *bilinear composition* implies the Bézier patch is a *tensor* (or *Cartesian*) *product*.

The four boundary curves are *P(s,0)* and *P(s,1)* for $s \in (0,1)$ and *P(0,t)* and *P(1,t)* for $t \in (0,1)$. The patch interpolates the four corner control points, but not the other 12. (Similarly, of the red curves in figure 18-3, the outer ones are coincident with the surface, but the inner ones are not.)

18.3 Continuity of Adjacent Bézier Patches

Internal to the patch, the surface is C^2 continuous. But continuity across the boundary of two Bézier patches must obey the constraints imposed for continuity of two Bézier curves (see section 16.6). For example, in the figure below, the four points that define the shared boundary between the two patches each should be at the midpoint of the green segment that connects control points across the patch boundary.

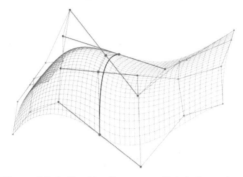

Figure 18-4: Continuity across Patch Boundary

In a memorable use of the continuity properties of the Bézier patch, in 1975, Martin Newell created the first computer graphics icon: the *Utah Teapot*. It can be seen below that the large (yellow and orange) patches meet with curvature continuity, and that the corresponding blue lines in the control mesh are colinear.

The teapot is a frequent test object, and in chapter 20 we'll use it to demonstrate the tessellation shader.

Figure 18-5: The Utah Teapot and Martin Newell
(used with permission)

18.4 The Surface Normal of a Bézier Patch

A point on a Bézier patch at parametric location (s, t) may be computed by a curve $B_s(t)$ in the s-direction or a curve $B_t(s)$ in the t-direction. That is, $P(s,t) = B_s(t) = B_t(s)$.

We can compute the tangents in the two directions, $B_s'(t)$ and $B_t'(s)$ using the method of section 16.2. The surface normal, then, is given by their cross-product.

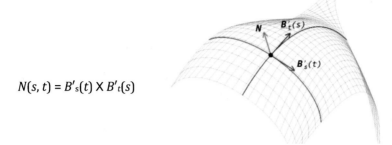

$$N(s, t) = B'_s(t) \times B'_t(s)$$

Figure 18-6: Surface normal of Bézier patch

18.5 Subdivision of the Bézier Patch

A Bézier patch can be subdivided with a method similar to the subdivision of the Bézier curve (sec. 16.4), in which four control points become seven, with the middle of the seven being shared between the two sub-curves.

If we regard the control mesh as spanning a square s X t space, with four s rows and four t columns, we can subdivide each row, producing a control mesh of 7 columns and 4 rows and a resulting pair of meshes that are C2-continuous along their shared boundary (which is defined by the middle of the 7 columns). Applying the subdivision to each of the columns results in a total of 49 control points defining four sub-patches.

In the subdivision illustrated below, the lower right sub-patch is manipulated with no effect on the other sub-patches. The entire surface remains C2-continuous.

Patch subdivision is sometimes used for rendering, but scan line methods are more common.

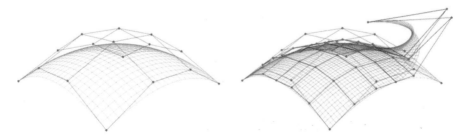

Figure 18-7: Subdivision of a Bézier patch
left: original patch, right: subdivided with manipulation

18.6 The Bézier Patch as a Matrix Product

We can restate section 18.2 more formally and compactly as a matrix. Recall that chapter 16 gives the Bézier curve in matrix form as:

$$P(s) = [s^3 \ s^2 \ s \ 1] \ [M] \begin{bmatrix} B_1 \\ B_2 \\ B_3 \\ B_4 \end{bmatrix},$$

$$\text{where } M = \begin{bmatrix} -1 & 3 & -3 & 1 \\ 3 & -6 & 3 & 0 \\ -3 & 3 & 0 & 0 \\ 1 & 0 & 0 & 0 \end{bmatrix} \text{ and } B_i \text{ are the four control points.}$$

Applying this to 16, not four, control points produces four points in the s-direction:

$$[P_{s1} \ P_{s2} \ P_{s3} \ P_{s4}] = [s^3 \ s^2 \ s \ 1] \ [M] \begin{bmatrix} B_{11} & B_{12} & B_{13} & B_{14} \\ B_{21} & B_{22} & B_{23} & B_{24} \\ B_{31} & B_{32} & B_{33} & B_{34} \\ B_{41} & B_{42} & B_{43} & B_{44} \end{bmatrix}$$

If we treat these four points as control points in the t-direction and evaluate them at t, the result is a single point at parametric location (s, t):

$$P_{st} = [t^3 \ t^2 \ t \ 1] \ [M] \begin{bmatrix} P_{s1} \\ P_{s2} \\ P_{s3} \\ P_{s4} \end{bmatrix}$$

Combining the above into a single equation:

$$P_{st} = [s^3 \ s^2 \ s \ 1] \ [M] \begin{bmatrix} B_{11} & B_{12} & B_{13} & B_{14} \\ B_{21} & B_{22} & B_{23} & B_{24} \\ B_{31} & B_{32} & B_{33} & B_{34} \\ B_{41} & B_{42} & B_{43} & B_{44} \end{bmatrix} [M]^T \begin{bmatrix} t^3 \\ t^2 \\ t \\ 1 \end{bmatrix}$$

If we represent the 16 control points as a matrix B, we can compute $C = [M][B][M]^T$, yielding:

$$P_{st} = [s^3 \ s^2 \ s \ 1] \ [C] \begin{bmatrix} t^3 \\ t^2 \\ t \\ 1 \end{bmatrix}$$

The elements of *C* are the cubic polynomial coefficients for the *x*, *y*, and *z* of the points on the patch. Because *M* is symmetric, i.e., $M = M^T$, *C* can be computed as follows:

```
vec3 ctrlPt[4][4];   // 16 Bezier control points, indexed [s][t]
vec3 coeff[4][4];    // 16 polynomial coefficients in x,y,z

void SetCoeffs() {
    // set Bezier coefficient matrix
    mat4 m(vec4(-1,3,-3,1),vec4(3,-6,3,0),vec4(-3,3,0,0),vec4(1,0,0,0));
    mat4 g;
    for (int k = 0; k < 3; k++)                    // separately x, y, z
        for (int i = 0; i < 16; i++)
            g[i/4][i%4] = ctrlPt[i/4][i%4][k];     // geometry matrix
        mat4 c = m*g*m;                            // coefficient matrix
        for (int i = 0; i < 16; i++)
            coeff[i/4][i%4][k] = c[i/4][i%4];      // xfer to 3D coeffs
    }
}
```

Thus, we have two methods to compute a point *P(s, t)* on a Bézier patch: using control points and five applications of the *BezierPoint* subroutine (see section 16.8), or using polynomial coefficients (which is more efficient):

```
vec3 PointFromCtrlPts(float s, float t) {
    vec3 spt[4];
    for (int i = 0; i < 4; i++) {
        int j = 4*i;
        spt[i]=BezierPoint(s,ctlPt[j][0],ctlPt[j][1],ctlPt[j][2],ctlPt[j][3]);
    }
    return BezierPoint(t, spt[0], spt[1], spt[2], spt[3]);
}

vec3 PointFromCoeffs(float s, float t) {
    vec3 p;
    float s2 = s*s, s3 = s*s2, t2 = t*t, ta[] = {t*t2, t2, t, 1};
    for (int i = 0; i < 4; i++) {
        int j = 4*i;
        p += ta[i]*(s3*coeff[j][0]+s2*coeff[j][1]+s*coeff[j][2]+coeff[j][3]);
    }
    return p;
}
```

18.7 Exercise

This exercise is to complete 18-StubBezierPatch.cpp. This includes calculating the point and normal given *u* and *v*, transferring vertex data to the GPU, drawing the patch, and drawing the control mesh.

The exercise can use the array of control points declared above. They can be initialized to default locations:

```
float vals[] = {-.75, -.25, .25, .75};
for (int i = 0; i < 4; i++)
    for (int j = 0; j < 4; j++)
        ctrlPts[i][j] = vec3(vals[i], vals[j], i%3==0||j%3==0? .5:0);
```

In the following subroutine we break the patch into quadrilaterals, *res* number in the *s*-direction and *res* number in the *t*-direction, for a total of res^2 quadrilaterals.

We compute the vertex data (location and normal) using *BezierPatch* (assumed to be either *PointFromCtrlPoints* or *PointFromCoeffs*, above). The data is written directly to the GPU vertex buffer using a pointer returned by *glMapBuffer*; this should not be called if the program is attempting to display from GPU memory, i.e., the following should not be called from within *Display*:

```
void SetVertices(int res, bool init = false) {
    // activate GPU vertex buffer
    glBindBuffer(GL_ARRAY_BUFFER, vBufferId);
    // get pointers to GPU memory for vertices, normals
    nQuadrilaterals = res*res;
    int sizeBuffer = 2*4*nQuadrilaterals*sizeof(vec3);
    if (init)
        glBufferData(GL_ARRAY_BUFFER, sizeBuffer, NULL, GL_STATIC_DRAW);
    vec3 *vPtr = (vec3 *) glMapBuffer(GL_ARRAY_BUFFER, GL_WRITE_ONLY);
    for (int i = 0; i < res; i++) {
        float s0 = (float) i/res, s1 = (float) (i+1)/res;
        for (int j = 0; j < res; j++) {
            float t0 = (float) j/res, t1 = (float) (j+1)/res;
            BezierPatch(s0, t0, vPtr, vPtr+1); vPtr += 2;
            BezierPatch(s1, t0, vPtr, vPtr+1); vPtr += 2;
            BezierPatch(s1, t1, vPtr, vPtr+1); vPtr += 2;
            BezierPatch(s0, t1, vPtr, vPtr+1); vPtr += 2;
        }
    }
    glUnmapBuffer(GL_ARRAY_BUFFER);
}
```

Or, we can save the vertices in CPU memory and then transfer to the GPU:

```
struct Vertex {
    vec3 point, normal;
    Vertex() { }
    Vertex(vec3 p, vec3 n) : point(p), normal(n) { }
};
```

159

```
void SetVertices(int res, bool init = false) {
    // activate GPU vertex buffer
    glBindBuffer(GL_ARRAY_BUFFER, vBufferId);
    int nQuadrilaterals = res*res;
    if (init) {
        // allocate GPU memory
        int sizeBuffer = 2*4*nQuadrilaterals*sizeof(vec3), vcount = 0;
        glBufferData(GL_ARRAY_BUFFER, sizeBuffer, NULL, GL_STATIC_DRAW);
    }
    // store points in dynamic array
    std::vector<Vertex> vertices(4*nQuadrilaterals);
    Vertex *v = &vertices[0];
    for (int i = 0; i < res; i++) {
        float s0 = (float) i/res, s1 = (float) (i+1)/res;
        for (int j = 0; j < res; j++) {
            float t0 = (float) j/res, t1 = (float) (j+1)/res;
            BezierPatch(s0, t0, &v->point, &v->normal); v++;
            BezierPatch(s1, t0, &v->point, &v->normal); v++;
            BezierPatch(s1, t1, &v->point, &v->normal); v++;
            BezierPatch(s0, t1, &v->point, &v->normal); v++;
        }
    }
    // transfer to GPU
    glBufferSubData(GL_ARRAY_BUFFER, 0, sizeBuffer, &vertices[0]);
}
```

The quadrilaterals are shaded with:

```
glDrawArrays(GL_QUADS, 0, 4*nQuadrilaterals);
```

Or, a line drawing can be made with:

```
for (int i = 0; i < nQuadrilaterals; i++)
    glDrawArrays(GL_LINE_LOOP, 4*i, 4);
```

18.8 NURBS Surfaces

Just as the B-spline class of curves includes the Bézier curve, the B-spline class of patches includes the Bézier patch. Non-Uniform Rational B-Spline patches are the preferred primitives for many computer-aided design systems. The mathematics is more complex but allows for forming certain surfaces (such as a hemi-sphere) that are not possible with non-rational methods. The Bézier patch, however, offers a more intuitive interaction with control points.

Further information about surface patches can be found in several texts, for example, *Computational Geometry for Design and Manufacture* by Faux and Pratt.

Chapter 19: The Geometry Shader

With OpenGLv3 (2008), an optional *geometry shader* was added to the graphics pipeline. This shader follows the vertex shader and precedes the rasterizer. It processes vertices like the vertex shader, but with three key differences:

1) Geometry shader inputs are arrays; this includes the built-in array *gl_in[]* as well as any explicitly defined arrays, such as:

```
in vec3 vPt[3];   // a triangle
```

Thus, the geometry shader gives the programmer access to the assembled primitive. This allows additional ('geometric') information to be computed and passed to the rasterizer, which can make qualitative improvements to an image. We hope to demonstrate these improvements in sec. 19-3.

The geometry shader supports points, lines, and triangles, but not quads. The size of the *vPt* input array can be explicitly given or determined from a layout parameter at the head of the shader, for example:

```
layout (triangles) in;
```

2) The geometry shader repeatedly writes to its output in order to form one or more primitives. The output consists of the built-in variable *gl_Position*, as well as any explicitly defined variables, such as:

```
out vec3 gPt;
out vec3 gColor;
```

Within a single call to the geometry shader, the output is generated multiple times, each time accompanied by the GLSL call:

```
EmitVertex();
```

Once *EmitVertex* has been called three times (for a triangle), a primitive is generated with the GLSL function:

```
EndPrimitive();
```

3) An arbitrary number of vertices may be emitted; that is, the geometry shader can output more primitives than it receives, thus increasing surface complexity.

19.1 Geometry Creation

Let's develop an example, 19-Demo-TriGeo.cpp, that demonstrates these features. We will render a tetrahedron, beginning with only three points that form an equilateral triangle in the *xy*-plane:

```
float h = 1/sqrt(3), pnts[][3] = {{.5f,-h/2,0},{0,h,0},{-.5,-h/2,0}};
glGenBuffers(1, &vBuffer);
glBindBuffer(GL_ARRAY_BUFFER, vBuffer);
glBufferData(GL_ARRAY_BUFFER, sizeof(pnts), &pnts[0], GL_STATIC_DRAW);
```

The vertex shader need only receive the points, transform them by the *modelview* matrix, and output them to the geometry shader:

```
const char *vertexShader = "\
    #version 330
    uniform mat4 modelview;
    in vec3 pt;
    out vec3 vPt;
    void main() {
        vPt = (modelview*vec4(pt, 1)).xyz;
    }";
```

The geometry shader receives the vertices in its *vPt* array. It defines a fourth vertex and then outputs four equilateral triangles, each of a different color, forming a tetrahedron:

```
void main() {
    vec3 center = (vPt[0]+vPt[1]+vPt[2])/3;
    vec3 n = normalize(cross(vPt[2]-vPt[1], vPt[1]-vPt[0]));
    float s = length(vPt[1]-vPt[0]);
    vec3 vPt3 = center+s*sqrt(2)/sqrt(3)*n;
    EmitTriangle(vPt[2], vPt[1], vPt[0], vec3(1,0,0)); // orig tri
    EmitTriangle(vPt[0], vPt[1], vPt3, vec3(0,1,0));   // new
    EmitTriangle(vPt[1], vPt[2], vPt3, vec3(0,0,1));   // new
    EmitTriangle(vPt[2], vPt[0], vPt3, vec3(0,1,1));   // new
}
```

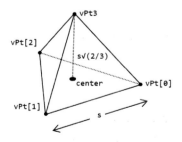

Figure 19-1: Forming a tetrahedron

EmitTriangle computes the triangle normal and outputs three points, each with a color, location, and (the same) normal (for a faceted appearance). *EmitVertex* and *EmitPrimitive* cause OpenGL to output the data from the geometry shader.

```
void EmitTriangle(vec3 p0, vec3 p1, vec3 p2, vec3 color) {
    gNrm = normalize(cross(v2-v1, v1-v0));
    for (int i = 0; i < 3; i++) {
        gColor = color;
        gPt = i==0? p0 : i==1? p1 : p2;
        gl_Position = persp*vec4(gPt, 1);
        EmitVertex();
    }
    EndPrimitive();
}
```

With the inclusion of this shader and a pixel shader that expects a point, normal, and color, a shaded tetrahedron rather than a single triangle will be displayed.

19.2 Exercise

Modify *main*, above, to produce an object other than a tetrahedron.

19.3 Line-on-Polygon Shading

We will now further develop 19-Demo-TriGeoShader so that it implements a recently developed method for line drawing. To put this in context, we offer a brief review.

A Trip Down Memory Line

The earliest computer graphic displays were *vector* (or, *calligraphic*). Programming usually consisted of a *MoveTo(p1)/DrawTo(p2)* pair of commands; analog electronics would then draw a line between *p1* and *p2*. Into the 1980s, video games were vector display; although unable to shade images, their lines were of high quality.

Raster line drawing initially involved setting pixels intersected by the line. Anti-aliasing was achieved if the pixel values depended on distance to the line and this was often calculated with incremental, pixel-to-pixel methods.

Line drawing remains popular for many tasks; for example, mesh structure can be better understood if facets are not only shaded but outlined as well. Yet something as basic as line-on-polygon had a fundamental problem. In pre-shader architecture, this was a two-pass method: a triangle was first shaded and then outlined.

For this to work, a small offset to the line's z-values was added to overcome the depth buffer values of the triangle (the offset must not be so great as to affect the visibility of the line with respect to other triangles). The resulting image is sensitive to the offset and can produce "z-fighting", in which the line fragments.

With the advent of the geometry shader, it became possible to shade a triangle and its outline at the same time by computing distance of the pixel from the nearest triangle edge. This technique derives from a 2006 SIGGRAPH "sketch" by Bærentzen et al., with implementation details from *OpenGL Shading Language Cookbook* by Wolff. Because it operates in a single pass, the technique is immune to z-fighting.

The pixel/edge distance calculations are performed in screen (pixel) space. As the inputs *p0*, *p1*, and *p2* have already been transformed by the *modelview* matrix, *EmitTriangle* need only transform them further by the perspective and viewport transformations. We send the viewport transformation to the geometry shader as a uniform, and compute the three screen-space points:

```
uniform mat4 viewport;

vec2 ScreenPoint(vec4 h) { return (viewport*vec4(h.xyz/h.w, 1)).xy;

// transform each vertex into screen space
vec2 s0 = ScreenPoint(persp*vec4(p0, 1))
vec2 s1 = ScreenPoint(persp*vec4(p1, 1))
vec2 s2 = ScreenPoint(persp*vec4(p2, 1))
```

Distance to an Edge

Bærentzen et al. used the geometry shader to compute the distance from each triangle vertex to its opposite edge (i.e., its *altitude*). We can store the distances in the variable *vec3 eDist* in which *eDist[0]*, *eDist[1]*, and *eDist[2]* are the distances to the edges opposite vertices *p0*, *p1*, and *p2*. Recalling that each vertex lies on two edges, *eDist* for vertices *p0*, *p1*, and *p2* are $(h_a, 0, 0)$, $(0, h_b, 0)$, and $(0, 0, h_c)$.

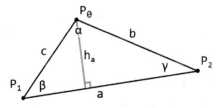

Figure 19-2: Altitude from *p0*

Angles *alpha* and *beta* can be computed with the Law of Cosines:

```
float a = length(s2-s1), b = length(s2-s0), c = length(s1-s0);
float alpha = acos((b*b+c*c-a*a)/(2*b*c));
float beta = acos((a*a+c*c-b*b)/(2*a*c));
```

From the two angles, we can compute the altitudes:

```
float ha = abs(c*sin(beta));   // screen-space distance p0 to p1p2
float hb = abs(c*sin(alpha));  // p1 to line p0p2
float hc = abs(b*sin(alpha));  // p2 to line p0p1
```

Finally, *EmitTriangle* needs a new output variable for the edge distances (i.e., altitudes):

```
noperspective out vec3 gEdgeDistance;
```

Before the call to *EmitVertex*, the edge distance triplet as well as the other vertex attributes are output for each vertex:

```
vec3 eDists[] = {vec3(ha, 0, 0), vec3(0, hb, 0), vec3(0, 0, hc)};
for (int i = 0; i < 3; i++) {
    gPt = i==0? p0 : i==1? p1 : p2;
    gl_Position = persp*vec4(gPt, 1);
    gEdgeDistance = eDists[i];
    EmitVertex();
}
```

For the pixel shader, a new input is needed:

```
noperspective in vec3 gEdgeDistance;
```

The *noperspective* keyword instructs the rasterizer not to apply the perspective divide to *gEdgeDistance*.

gEdgeDistance provides accurate screen-space distance between the pixel and the three triangle edges because point-to-line distance is a linear function that remains accurate under bilinear interpolation by the rasterizer.

For a given pixel, to find the distance to the nearest triangle edge, we merely find the minimum element in gEdgeDistance:

```
// get distance to nearest edge and map to 0,1
float minD = min(min(gEdgeDist[0], gEdgeDist[1]), gEdgeDist[2]);
```

We can use the GLSL subroutine *smoothstep* to map *minD* to the interval (0,1), assuming *minD* is within the "transition zone" between shade color and line color. If *minD* is beyond the zone, *t* is 1 (fully inside triangle); if it is below the zone, *t* is 0 (fully within line):

```
float t = smoothstep(width-transition, width+transition, minD);
```

smoothstep is "smooth" because it is a continuous function between a minimum (i.e., *width-transition*) and maximum (i.e, *width+transition*), its derivative at the two endpoints is zero.

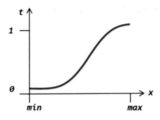

Figure 19-3: *smoothstep(min, max, x)*

Given the parameter *t*, we can combine the line color (black in the code below) and the shade color (*gColor*, assumed to be a shader input) with the *mix* function, such that when *t* is 0 the color is that of the line, and when *t* is 1 it is that of the shade color:

```
pColor = mix(vec4(0,0,0,1), vec4(intensity*gColor,1), t);
```

We can produce a line drawing, i.e., no shading, only if we disable the *z*-buffer, skip the shading intensity calculation, and simply assign pColor = vec4(0,0,0,1-t). Or we can produce hidden line elimination (with *z*-buffer enabled) by assigning pColor = vec4(t,t,t,1).

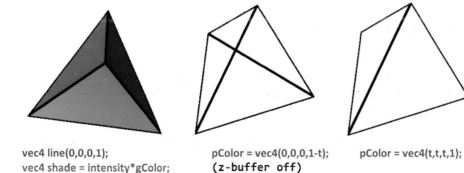

vec4 line(0,0,0,1);   pColor = vec4(0,0,0,1-t);   pColor = vec4(t,t,t,1);
vec4 shade = intensity*gColor;   (z-buffer off)
pColor = mix(line, shade, t);

Figure 19-4: Result and variations

A magnified view reveals a problem with silhouette edges: they are not anti-aliased along their outer edge, and the line is half as thick.

Figure 19-5: Silhouette and non-silhouette edges

By an extended arrangement of the triangle array, not only the primitive but its neighbors become accessible in the geometry shader. This allows, for example, cartoon shading or silhouette-only shading.

Access to a triangle's neighbors is achieved with *glDrawElements*. Rather than an integer array of triangle indices (every three constituting a triangle), it is passed an array of six indices that define a triangle and its neighbors, per the diagram below. To obtain this behavior, the first argument to *glDrawElements* must be GL_TRIANGLES_ADJACENCY.

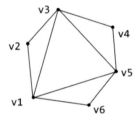

Figure 19-6: Triangle v1v3v5 and adjacent triangles

This access to neighbor triangles can rectify the staircasing in figure 19-5.

In the next chapter we will use this line-drawing geometry shader to illustrate tessellation of a Bézier patch.

19.4 Exercise

Apply the method in the previous section to draw silhouette edges only.

Chapter 20: Tessellation

With version 4.0 (released in 2010), OpenGL added two *tessellation shaders* to the graphics pipeline: the *tessellation control* shader and the *tessellation evaluation* shader. Like the geometry shader, they are optional. The entire pipeline of shaders (except the rasterizer) is programmable.

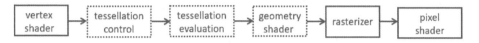

Figure 20-1: Modern graphics pipeline

The tessellation evaluation shader allocates additional vertices in order to partition primitives (triangles and quadrilaterals) into sub-primitives (always triangles), which are then passed to the rasterizer (or, if present, to the geometry shader).

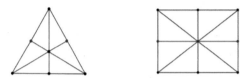

Figure 20-2: Simple triangle and quad tessellation

The partitioning resolution is governed by 'inner' and 'outer' parameters, which refer to the number of divisions internal to the primitive and the number along the edge of the primitive. These parameters can be set in the tessellation control shader, or explicitly set by the application. We'll consider tessellation evaluation first, and return to tessellation control later in this chapter.

With the tessellation shader, the computation of the new vertices is confined to the GPU, and the enumeration of additional triangles is managed by OpenGL. That is, tessellation increases vertex resolution without requiring the application to represent the additional vertices or organize them into primitives. This simplifies programming and reduces CPU/GPU transfers.

As with the geometry shader, the tessellation shader receives vertex attributes in the form of input arrays and, like the geometry shader, defines new vertices while able to access the entire, enclosing primitive. There is no need, however, for *EmitVertex* and *EndPrimitive*.

Macro and Micro Geometric Displacement

 The increased vertex resolution allows geometry to be modified at the micro and macro levels.

For example, at the micro level, the tessellation shader, used in conjunction with a depth map, can create surface geometry that approximates the geometry used to calculate the bump (normal) map (see sec 14.1). This improves the realistic appearance of silhouette edges and permits a bump to occlude other bumps.

As an example, consider a depth map of a penny, and its use for bump mapping and displacement mapping, below. The underlying displacement grid is 60 by 60.

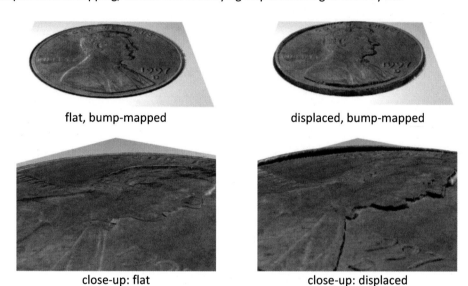

flat, bump-mapped   displaced, bump-mapped

close-up: flat   close-up: displaced

Figure 20-3: Bump-mapped and displacement-mapped
(depth and texture data courtesy Gene Cooper)

At the macro level, an entire object can be defined. In this chapter, we'll look at examples in which a tessellation shader converts a single quad into a height field, a sphere, and a Bézier patch.

We'll combine the macro and micro to render an image of Earth. The tessellater will convert the quad to a sphere at the macro level. At the micro level, it will displace the spherical surface using a depth (or *elevation*) map to simulate mountains.

The use of *displacement maps* was demonstrated in Cook's 1984 paper, *Shade Trees*.

Changes to Display

Tessellation is initiated in OpenGL when an application calls *glDrawArrays*, with the first argument (GL_POINTS/LINES/TRIANGLES/QUADS) replaced with GL_PATCHES. The patch may be 3 or 4 sided, but the tessellation will produce triangles.

For example, to tessellate a quad:

```
glPatchParameteri(GL_PATCH_VERTICES, 4);   // patch is four-sided
glDrawArrays(GL_PATCHES, 0, 4);            // draw one 4-sided patch
```

If we wish to skip the control tessellation shader, the resolution can be set to *r* in *Display* by passing two floating-point arrays to OpenGL:

```
float outerLevels[] = {r, r, r, r}, innerLevels[] = {r, r};
    // defined as floats, but intended use is integer
glPatchParameterfv(GL_PATCH_DEFAULT_OUTER_LEVEL, outerLevels);
glPatchParameterfv(GL_PATCH_DEFAULT_INNER_LEVEL, innerLevels);
```

These *innerLevels* and *outerLevels* arrays control the partitioning of the patch so that adjacent patches share vertices (and thereby avoid cracks along their boundaries).

For the initial examples we set all elements in the two arrays (*outerLevels* and *innerLevels*) to the same value, dividing a quad into $(r-1)^2$ sub-quads. In sec. 20.6, we'll use a tessellation control shader so that a quad's resolution is proportional to its screen size.

Evaluation

To execute, a tessellation evaluation shader must be compiled and linked to the GLSL program. The examples in the next few sections use a fixed resolution.

In our quad examples, the tessellation evaluation shader computes vertex locations and other vertex attributes needed by the pixel shader. This replaces the function of the vertex shader and eliminates the need for a vertex buffer.

A vertex shader must be compiled and linked, however, although as a no-op:

```
const char *vShaderCode = "
    #version 400 core
    void main() {
        gl_Position = vec4(0);
    }";
```

When the tessellater needs an additional vertex, it executes the evaluation shader, providing the appropriate (u, v) coordinates in the form of the built-in variable *gl_TessCoord*.

The *modelView* and *persp* transformations normally performed by the vertex shader are performed by the tessellation evaluation shader. The outputs *tePoint*, *teNormal*, and *teUv* replace those of the vertex shader.

The tessellation shader specifies "quads" (as a 'layout' parameter) as the basic geometry to be partitioned. "triangles" and "isolines", described later in the chapter, are two other tessellation types supported by OpenGLv4.

20.1 Tessellation of a Quad

A quadrilateral is naturally parameterized over the domain [0,1] X [0,1]. That is, OpenGL tessellates a quad by spanning the *uv* (or 'texture') parametric space, with *u* and *v* ranging 0 through 1. The specification of (u, v) coordinates for a triangle is more complicated and is discussed at the end of this chapter.

In this section, we'll tessellate a height field, a mountainous globe, and a Bézier patch.

Tessellation of a Height Field

Displacement based upon a height map combined with tessellation is a convenient mechanism to create terrain. As an example, we'll define Yosemite Valley from publicly available elevation data.

The height map is treated like a texture map; the uniform *heightfield* is set by the application in the same way as it would set a texture map (see section 12.4). The uniform *heightScale* controls the degree of displacement (defaulting to none).

The quad defaults to a square in the *xy*-plane. The normal of such a quad is (0,0,1) and so the displacement is in that direction, by an amount dependent on the value of the height field at the given (u, v). The resulting point and the normal are then transformed by the matrices and output. The *uv*-coordinates are also output.

```
const char *teShaderCode = "\
    #version 400 core
    layout (quads, equal_spacing, ccw) in;
    uniform mat4 modelview;
    uniform mat4 persp;
    uniform sampler2D heightField;
    uniform float heightScale = 0;
    out vec3 tePoint;
```

```
out vec3 teNormal;
out vec2 teUv;
void main() {
    teUv = gl_TessCoord.st;
    vec3 p = vec3(-1+2*teUv.s, -1+2*teUv.t, 0);   // spans [-1,1]
    vec3 n = vec3(0, 0, 1);
    float height = texture(heightField, teUv).r;
    p += heightScale*height*n;
    tePoint = (modelview*vec4(p, 1)).xyz;
    teNormal = (modelview*vec4(n, 0)).xyz;
    gl_Position = persp*vec4(tePoint, 1);
}";
```

In the following example, a height field of Yosemite Valley displaces a tessellated quad. A normal (bump) map derived from the height field is applied in the pixel shader, as in sec. 14.5. A satellite view of the valley provides a texture map. Three lights illuminate.

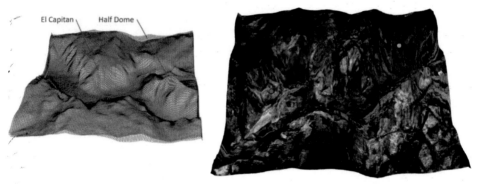

Figure 20-4: Tessellation of quad using Yosemite Valley height field and texture map

Effect on the Surface Normal

The height field (or depth map) raises issues concerning the surface normal. The tessellation shader can approximate the surface normal with central differences, but pre-computing a normal map is more efficient. These pre-computed normals need adjustment depending on the degree of displacement.

As noted in chapter 14, the derivation of the normal map from a height field implies a relationship of scale between the depth image and the variation in depth. Bump-mapping is applied to a flat surface so that no adjustment to the surface normals obtained from the normal map are warranted for a surface displaced less than the nominal amount implied by *pixelScale* (see section 14.1).

If the surface is displaced by a greater amount, however, a vertical exaggeration occurs to the surface that is not captured by the original normal map. In such cases, a vertical scaling in *z* of the normal (followed by unitization) can compensate.

Exercise

Create a terrain from a single quad and a height field. Use GoogleMaps (satellite view) to snap a texture, and find *Heightmapper* on the web to snap a depth map of the same terrain. Then, make a 3D image using displacement mapping, bump mapping, and texture mapping.

20.2 Tessellation of a Sphere

A sphere can be tessellated beginning with a single quad, simply by treating (*u, v*) coordinates as longitude and latitude. The previous example can be modified so that the surface point *p* and surface normal *n* are computed with:

```
float u = teUv.s, v = teUv.t; // longitude, latitude
float _PI = 3.141592;
float elevation = _PI/2-_PI*v;
float eFactor = cos(elevation);
float y = sin(elevation);
float angle = 2*_PI*(u);
float x = eFactor*cos(angle), z = eFactor*sin(angle);
p = vec3(x, y, z);
n = p;                          // for unit sphere, normal = position
```

To simulate a mountainous Earth, a depth map displaces the location obtained by the sphere function. A normal ('bump') map (derived from the depth map) modifies the normal during shading, and a texture map is applied for coloring.

Figure 20-5: Texture, depth, and normal maps (first two freely available from NASA)

The texture and bump maps are applied at pixel resolution, whereas the displacement map is applied at tessellation resolution.

texture-mapped globe   and bump-mapped   & displacement-mapped

Figure 20-6: Mappings applied to a sphere

Exercise

Part A: modify the sphere function of (*u*, *v*) to produce a cylinder.
Part B: modify the function to produce a torus.

In both, use texture and/or depth maps other than Earth.

20.3 Tessellation of a Bézier Patch

In exercise 18-7, a Bézier patch is triangulated by the application into vertices that are stored in the GPU. Whenever the user modifies one of the patch control points, the patch is retriangulated and the new vertices are transferred to the GPU.

With the tessellation evaluation shader, no GPU vertex buffer is used and no *SetVertices* subroutine is needed. When the user moves a control point, the application transfers a new set of control points (as an input uniform) to the GPU. The tessellation evaluation shader computes the positions and surface normals from (*u*, *v*) locations provided by the tessellation mechanism.

Rather than use the more efficient coefficient evaluation (sec. 18.6), the following shader implements the evaluation in terms of an *s*-curve and *t*-curve; this provides a simple means to compute the surface normal:

```
char *teShaderCode = "
  #version 400 core
  layout (quads, equal_spacing, ccw) in;
  uniform vec3 ctrlPts[16]; // 16 control pts updated on user move
  uniform mat4 modelview;   // object to eye space
  uniform mat4 persp;       // eye space to perspective space
  out vec3 tePoint;         // generated point at (s,t)
  out vec3 teNormal;        // generated normal at (s,t)
  out vec2 teUv;            // same as (s,t)
```

```
vec3 BezTangent(float t, vec3 b1, vec3 b2, vec3 b3, vec3 b4) {
  float t2 = t*t;
  return (-3*t2+6*t-3)*b1+(9*t2-12*t+3)*b2+(6*t-9*t2)*b3+3*t2*b4;
}
vec3 BezPoint(float t, vec3 b1, vec3 b2, vec3 b3, vec3 b4) {
  // equation 16.1
  float t2 = t*t, t3 = t*t2;
  return (-t3+3*t2-3*t+1)*b1+(3*t3-6*t2+3*t)*b2+(3*t2-3*t3)*b3+t3*b4;
}
void main() {
  vec3 spts[4], tpts[4];
  float s = gl_TessCoord.st.s, t = gl_TessCoord.st.t;
  teUv = vec2(s, t);
  for (int i = 0; i < 4; i++) {
    spts[i] = BezPoint(s, ctrlPts[4*i], ctrlPts[4*i+1],
                          ctrlPts[4*i+2],ctrlPts[4*i+3]);
    tpts[i] = BezPoint(t, ctrlPts[i], ctrlPts[i+4],
                          ctrlPts[i+8], ctrlPts[i+12]);
  }
  vec3 p = BezPoint(t, spts[0], spts[1], spts[2], spts[3]);
  vec3 tTan = BezTangent(t, spts[0], spts[1], spts[2], spts[3]);
  vec3 sTan = BezTangent(s, tpts[0], tpts[1], tpts[2], tpts[3]);
  vec3 n = normalize(cross(sTan, tTan));
  tePoint = (modelview*vec4(p, 1)).xyz;     // eye space point
  teNormal = (modelview*vec4(n, 0)).xyz;    // eye space normal
  gl_Position = persp*vec4(tePoint, 1);     // persp space point
}";
```

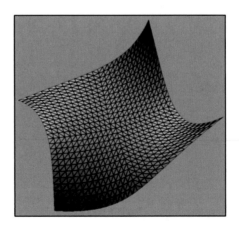

Figure 20-7: Tessellated Bézier patch

175

Exercise 1

Modify exercise 18.7 to use the above tessellation evaluation shader.

Exercise 2

Render the Utah Teapot, using the control points and patches defined in 20-Stub-Teapot.cpp.

20.4 Tessellation of a Bézier Curve

In the examples in chapters 16 (parametric curves) and 17 (text), a curve is drawn when the application, i.e., the CPU, computes points. The curve can, however, be tessellated and drawn by the GPU, using the tessellation layout parameter 'isolines'.

To render a curve as *res* number of line segments, add the following to *Display*:

```
float innerLevels[] = {res, res}, outerLevels[] = {1, res, 1, 1};
glPatchParameterfv(GL_PATCH_DEFAULT_OUTER_LEVEL, outerLevels);
glPatchParameterfv(GL_PATCH_DEFAULT_INNER_LEVEL, innerLevels);
```

and continue to call glDrawArrays(GL_PATCHES, 0, 4)

The tessellation shader below is sent four control points, and the value of the curve is computed given *gl_TessCoord.st.s* supplied by the tessellater.

```
char *teShaderCode = "
   #version 400 core
   layout (isolines, equal_spacing) in;
   uniform vec3 ctrlPts[4];
   uniform mat4 view;
   vec3 BezPoint(float t, vec3 b1, vec3 b2, vec3 b3, vec3 b4) {
       float t2 = t*t, t3 = t*t2;
       return (-t3+3*t2-3*t+1)*b1+(3*t3-6*t2+3*t)*b2+(3*t2-3*t3)*b3+t3*b4;
   }
   void main() {
       float s = gl_TessCoord.st.s;
       vec3 p = BezPoint(s, ctrlPts[0], ctrlPts[1], ctrlPts[2], ctrlPts[3]);
       gl_Position = view*vec4(p, 1);
   }";
```

20.5 Extending Tessellation Resolution

Displacement is one method to increase the realism of silhouette edges. Bump-mapping and texture-mapping are typically at much higher resolutions, however. The number of vertices generated by a tessellater is on the order of hundreds or thousands. OpenGL has a built-in limit that can be queried, but the actual number supported is hardware-dependent. A typical limit as of this writing is 64 by 64 (i.e., less than 5000 vertices).

This resolution does not prevent the artifacts visible along ridges of the ripples in the middle of the following figure. To reduce the aliasing, the application could blur the depth map (but not the normal map derived from the original depth map) or, equivalently, use *textureLod* in the pixel shader to freeze the mipmap level.

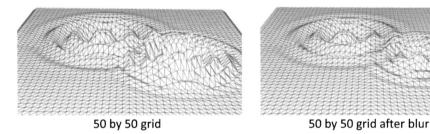

| 50 by 50 grid | 50 by 50 grid after blur |

Figure 20-8: Low resolution and effect of blur

In the case of the quad, improvement is possible by tessellating multiple sub-quads. The quad tessellation shaders in this chapter are driven solely by *uv*-coordinates, so it is a simple matter to partition the initial quad.

First, two uniform inputs are added to the tessellation shader:

```
uniform vec2 uvOffset = vec2(0, 0);
uniform float uvScale = 1;
```

and the assignment to **teUv** is modified:

```
teUv = uvOffset+uvScale*gl_TessCoord.st;
```

The original quad can be displayed as *nQuadsOnEdge* by *nQuadsOnEdge* sub-quads with this code in *Display*:

```
int nQuadsOnEdge = 2;        // 4 sub-quads
float uvScale = 1.f/nQuadsOnEdge;
SetUniform(shader, "uvScale", uvScale);
for (int i = 0; i < nQuadsOnEdge; i++)
    for (int j = 0; j < nQuadsOnEdge; j++) {
        SetUniform(shader, "uvOffset", uvScale*vec2(i, j));
        glDrawArrays(GL_PATCHES, 0, 4);
    }
```

177

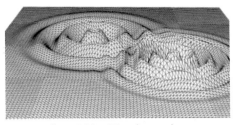 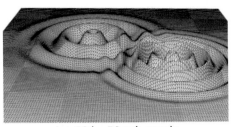

four 50 by 50 sub-quads   nine 50 by 50 sub-quads

Figure 20-9: Effect of extended resolution

20.6 Level of Detail

We now return to the tessellation control shader. With it we can control the resolution of the tessellation evaluation shader in response to display conditions. This provides a generic mechanism to control *level of detail*.

The shader specifies dual resolutions for a primitive: an *inner* and an *outer*. The inner is the basic resolutioin for subdivision, but the outer represents a "fringe" that allows an edge of the subdivided primitive to match an adjoining subdivided primitive of a different, inner resolution.

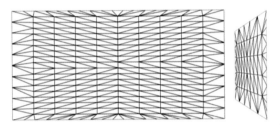

Figure 20-10: Effect of tessellation control shader on a differently oriented patch

In 20-Demo-BezierLOD, the tessellation control shader sets the four outer resolutions proportional to the screen space distance between corners of the control mesh. The inner resolutions are set to the average of their corresponding outer resolutions. Adjoining meshes might have different inner resolutions, but should have the same outer resolution along their shared boundary.

In the following example of a tessellation control shader, the tessellation resolutions are set only on the first call of the frame:

```
// tessellation control
const char *tcShaderCode = "\
#version 400 core
```

178

```
layout (vertices = 4) out;
uniform vec3 ctrlPts[16];
uniform int minTessLevel = 10;
uniform int maxTessLevel = 50;
uniform mat4 modelview;
uniform mat4 persp;
void main() {
  if (gl_InvocationID == 0) {  // only set once per frame display
      mat4 m = persp*modelview;
      // test distance bet pairs of corner ctrl pts
      vec3 corners[] = {ctrlPts[0][0], ctrlPts[0][3],
                        ctrlPts[3][3], ctrlPts[3][0]};
      vec2 scorners[4]; // screen space
      for (int i = 0; i < 4; i++) {
          vec4 h = m*vec4(corners[i], 1);
          scorners[i] = h.xy/h.w;
      }
      // set inner res to max res of 4 outer edges
      gl_TessLevelInner[0] = 0;
      for (int i = 0; i < 4; i++) {
          float d = distance(scorners[i], scorners[(i+1)%4]);
          float l = gl_TessLevelOuter[i] = max(2, 4*d);
          if (l > gl_TessLevelInner[0])
              gl_TessLevelInner[0] = gl_TessLevelInner[1] = 1;
      }
}";
```

20.7 Tessellation of a Triangular Mesh

The previous examples have used a single quad to define geometry, with a new vertex specified with *gl_tessCoord.st*. In the case of a triangle, however, a new vertex must be specified in terms of the three triangle corners, creating a *trilinear interpolation*. The interpolation coefficients (also called *barycentric coordinates*) are applied to the triangle corners to compute a *weighted sum* (nominally, these coefficients sum to 1).

Whereas *gl_TessCoord.st* provides coordinates for a new quad vertex, *gl_TessCoord.stp* provides coordinates for a new triangle vertex.

Vertex location, normal, texture coordinates, and local texture axes are stored in the vertex buffer, as described in sec. 14.3. They are sent to the vertex shader, but merely passed, without transformation, to the tessellation shader as input arrays of three:

```
layout (triangles, fractional_odd_spacing, ccw) in;
in vec3 vPoint[];
in vec3 vNormal[];
in vec2 vUv[];
in vec3 vUaxis[];
in vec3 vVaxis[];
out vec3 tePoint;
```

```
out vec3 teNormal;
out vec2 teUv;
out vec3 teUaxis;
out vec3 teVaxis;
```

Unlike with Bézier patch rendering, local coordinate frames must be computed for use in displacement-mapping and bump-mapping (see section 14.6). Thus, the new vertex location, normal, *uv*-coordinates, and local tangents are computed as a weighted sum with the following loop through the triangle corners:

```
vec2 t;
vec3 p, n, ua, va;          // location, normal, u-axis, v-axis
for (int i = 0; i < 3; i++) {
    float f = gl_TessCoord[i];
    p += f*tcPoint[i];
    n += f*tcNormal[i];
    t += f*tcUv[i];
    ua += f*tcUaxis[i];
    va += f*tcVaxis[i];
}
```

p may now be displaced along the surface normal given a displacement map (sec. 20.1); it is then transformed by *modelview*. Results are output for the rasterizer:

```
tePoint = (modelview*vec4(p, 1)).xyz;
teNormal = (modelview*vec4(n, 0)).xyz;
teUaxis = (modelview*vec4(ua, 0)).xyz;
teVaxis = (modelview*vec4(va, 0)).xyz;
teUv = t;
gl_Position = persp*vec4(tePoint, 1);
```

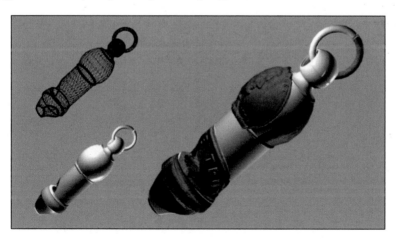

Figure 20-11: Left: line-drawn and single-shaded mesh
right: displacement-mapped, bump-mapped, and texture-mapped mesh

Meshes with Openings

In chapter 15 we defined a mesh with an opening as having at least one edge that is shared by only one triangle (or quad). The above whistle is such a mesh; its mouth allows the 'inside' to be seen, so culling back-face triangles (sec. 15-4) will not work..

This raises a question concerning rendering a back-facing primitive. We expect to illuminate it by the same light sources as the rest of the mesh, but the back-facing primitives face, roughly, in the opposite direction as do the front-faces.

This is usually solved by a two-pass method, doubling the render time: first the back-facing primitives are rendered with negated surface normals. Then, front-facing primitives are rendered with unnegated normals:

```
glEnable(GL_CULL_FACE);
glFrontFace(GL_CW);
SetUniform(shaderId, "reverseNormals", 1);
glDrawArrays(GL_TRIANGLES, 0, 3*triangles.size());
glFrontFace(GL_CCW);
SetUniform(shaderId, "reverseNormals", 0);
glDrawArrays(GL_TRIANGLES, 0, 3*triangles.size());
```

We can, however, perform this task in one pass with a tessellation or geometry shader. Both give access to the entire primitive, so it is straightforward to compute back-facing:

```
vec3 p0 = (modelview*vec4(vPoint[0], 1)).xyz;
vec3 p1 = (modelview*vec4(vPoint[1], 1)).xyz;
vec3 p2 = (modelview*vec4(vPoint[2], 1)).xyz;
bool backfacing = cross(p1-p0, p2-p1).z < 0;
```

If the mesh has a reasonable *uv*-parameterization, it is also possible to compute back-facing in the pixel shader by first computing the local *u-axis* and *v-axis* (sec. 15-3), and testing the *z*-component of their cross product.

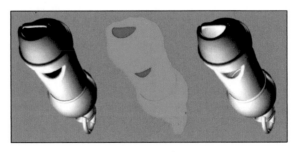

Figure 20-12: Left to right: unlighted back-faces, back-face detection, lighted back-faces

Chapter 21: Animation

Computer animation was first demonstrated by Ed Catmull and Fred Parke at the University of Utah in 1974; Catmull animated a hand and Parke animated faces. These productions overcame numerous technical challenges while maintaining a degree of artistic control.

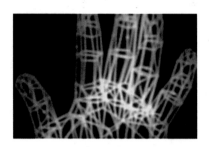 

Figure 21-1: First Computer Animations
(courtesy Ed Catmull and Fred Parke)

The first major contribution of 3D computer graphics to theatrical motion pictures was the Genesis Sequence in *Wrath of Khan*, 1982. Since the fully computer-generated T-Rex in *Jurassic Park*, 1993, computer imagery in movies has been common.

21.1 Principles of Animation

The Illusion of Life, by Disney animators Frank Thomas and Ollie Johnston, describes twelve *principles of animation*. They are:

Squash and Stretch,
Anticipation,
Staging,
Straight Ahead and Pose-To-Pose Action,
Follow Through and Overlapping Action,
Slow In and Slow Out,
Arcs,
Secondary Action,
Timing,
Exaggeration,
Solid Drawing, and
Appeal.

In 1984, John Lasseter joined the Lucasfilm graphics group (to become Pixar in 1986), bringing with him an adherence to these principles. In a 1987 SIGGRAPH paper, he described their use in defining the *personality* of Luxo, Jr., the title character in Pixar's award-winning short animation.

Pixar has pioneered many computer animation techniques. In 2014, Ed Catmull published *Creative, Inc.*, an account of his efforts to maintain the quality of Pixar animations after the success of *Toy Story*, and, eventually, to revitalize Disney Animation Studios.

21.2 Character Rigging and Key Frames

Figure 21-2: A homunculus

An animation's enactment requires the placement and orientation of numerous elements, including the camera, lights, props, and characters.

A character is often represented geometrically as a hierarchy of sub-models (think knee-bone connected to the thigh-bone). A sub-model is defined in an 'object space' and transformed into a scene according to an associated position and orientation, i.e., a *reference frame*. This can be represented by a matrix:

$$\begin{bmatrix} v1_x & v2_x & v3_x & p_x \\ v1_y & v2_y & v3_y & p_y \\ v1_z & v2_z & v3_z & p_z \\ 0 & 0 & 0 & 1 \end{bmatrix}$$

where *p* is the location of the frame, and the three vectors *v1*, *v2*, and *v3* define its orientation.

Consider this simple arm model defined by three reference frames located at the shoulder (F_1), the elbow (F_2), and wrist (F_3).

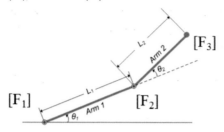

Figure 21-3: Reference frames along an articulated arm

For a model at rest, the relationship between parent and child reference frames can be expressed as a transformation applied at the *joint*. For example, the orientation of the shoulder joint determines the location of the elbow; the relationship between the shoulder and elbow can be given by a transformation matrix T_1, where $T_1 = F_2 F_1^{-1}$.

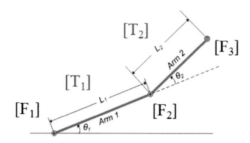

Figure 21-4: Reference frames and transformations

Characters can be animated by changing the transformation matrices T_i over time. When T_1 is modified, F_2 may be updated to $F_1 T_1$ (and subsequently F_3 may be updated to $F_2 T_2$).

The mechanism used by an animator to control these changes is known as *rigging*. With it, animators create 'key frames', i.e., a set of transformation matrices and reference frames for each key moment in the animation. There are several, general methods for rigging.

21.3 Kinematics and Motion Capture

Forward kinematics is direct control over the transformation matrices. As a particular T_i is adjusted by the user, the dependent reference frames F_i in the hierarchy are recomputed, and the object redisplayed. To adjust a reference frame, the *Mover* in Widgets.h could be augmented with an *Aimer*.

This direct control is often in the form of Euler angles (see sec. 6.6). Control can become difficult, however, if a rotation causes an axis to align with an original axis, a condition known as 'gimbal lock'.

Inverse kinematics is the automatic calculation of transformations given the location of an 'end effector'. That is, the user positions a sub-model, say the tip of a finger, and those transformation matrices between the object's base and the fingertip are recomputed (subject to various constraints). Not only is this computationally more demanding, but, if there are more than a couple of joints, the system is under-defined, meaning there are multiple combinations that produce the same end result. If care is not taken, unwanted or unexpected joint angles can result.

Alternatively, the transformation matrices T can be ignored by directly setting the reference frames F through *motion capture*.

21.4 Intermediate Frames

Once an animator has established key reference frames, intermediate reference frames are computed when the animation is rendered. For time t, a reference frame is interpolated between the bracketing key frames (the ones nearest in time before and after t).

An interpolated reference frame cannot be computed by interpolating individual matrix elements (as this would violate several trigonometric relations). An alternative approach is to extract *Euler angles* from the reference frame matrices and interpolate them to create new frames. (A better approach is described in the next chapter.)

21.5 Exercise: Animate

Create an animation using a mechanism similar to exercise 5.3 (a rotating letter) in which one or more principles of animation are utilized.

The application could read a mesh from a file, similar to exercise 15.5, and animate it through a transformation matrix that varies with time. Or, animate Bézier control points. Or, animate any object you can define and display.

The objective of this exercise is to incorporate one or more animation principles. For example, if a mesh is to be rendered, its vertices can be transformed by a matrix that implements a) squash and stretch (by differential scaling), b) arcs (by translation), or c) exaggeration/appeal as a function of the matrix. Any motion can be modified by applying a) timing, b) anticipation, c) slow-in-and-out through arbitrarily complex functions of elapsed time.

Or, move the camera along a curve that interpolates key camera frames.

Imagine.

Chapter 22: Quaternions

The Euler angles described in chapter 5 are often used to specify a reference frame; but the reverse is problematic: the extraction of angles from a reference frame is ill-defined and can yield unintended results.

Furthermore, the interpolation of Euler angles does not yield a rotation about a constant axis; rather, the axis wobbles. In the following figure are two reference frames, XYZ and X'Y'Z' (the latter is the former rotated 90° about the z-axis and then 90° about the y-axis). Interpolating the Euler angles produces sweeps from X to X' (in red), Y to Y' (green) and Z to Z' (blue). The X and Y sweeps are not planar, thus the wobble.

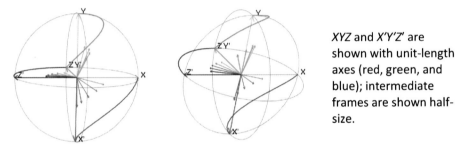

XYZ and X'Y'Z' are shown with unit-length axes (red, green, and blue); intermediate frames are shown half-size.

Figure 22-1 Euler angle interpolation, oblique view (left) and side view

22.1 Euler's Formula: Rotation as Complex Multiplication

Compared with Euler angles, it is computationally robust and geometrically correct to use *quaternions*. These were developed as an extension of complex numbers.

A complex number $(a + bi)$ is specified by a real coordinate a and an imaginary coordinate b, where i is the *imaginary unit* (i.e., $i^2 = -1$). Given two complex numbers, $(a + bi)$ and $(c + di)$, their product $(a + bi)(c + di)$ is defined as $(ac - bd) + (ad + bc)i$.

$(a + bi)$ can be visualized as a point on a *complex plane* defined by a real axis *Re* and an imaginary axis *Im*.

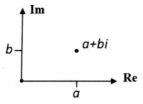

Figure 22-2: A number in the complex plane

If we consider the unit circle in the complex plane, a fundamental relationship is given by *Euler's Formula*:

(22-1) $e^{i\theta} = \cos\theta + i\sin\theta$

That is, $e^{i\theta}$ is a complex number whose real coordinate is cos(θ) and whose imaginary coordinate is sin(θ).

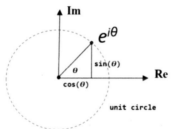

Figure 22-3: Euler's Formula in the complex plane

Euler's Formula readily shows that multiplication by a complex number performs a rotation; that is, when two exponentials are multiplied, their exponents sum, as do the corresponding angles of rotation.

(22-2) $e^{i\theta}\,e^{i\Phi} = e^{i(\theta+\Phi)} = \cos(\theta+\Phi) + i\sin(\theta+\Phi)$

Expanding the left side of 22.2 derives the angle sum identities of chapter 5:

$\cos(\theta+\Phi) + i\sin(\theta+\Phi) = e^{i\theta}e^{i\Phi} = (\cos\theta + i\sin\theta)(\cos\Phi + i\sin\Phi)$
$= \cos\theta\cos\Phi - \sin\theta\sin\Phi + i(\cos\theta\sin\Phi + \sin\theta\cos\Phi)$

The angle a between the axis Re and the line from the origin to a complex number z is called the *argument* of z. It follows from Euler's Formula that the argument of the product is the sum of the multiplicand arguments. Thus, a complex number is a rotation operator.

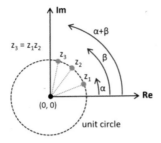

For points off the unit circle, the angular relationships hold, but the result's distance to the origin is the product of the multiplicands' distances, i.e., $|z_3| = |z_1||z_2|$.

Figure 22-4: Multiplication of complex numbers

Legendary physicist Richard Feynman called Euler's Formula "the most remarkable formula in mathematics".

Figure 22-5: Leonhard Euler

22.2 Extension to Three Dimensions

In 1843, William Hamilton extended complex multiplication beyond the two-dimensional complex plane by replacing the imaginary axis **Im** with three imaginary axes **I**, **J**, and **K**, while retaining the real axis **Re**. He grouped the scalars associated with the four axes into a 4-tuple he named 'quaternion'.

Quaternions have been used since the 1960s to calculate spaceflight trajectories. In 1985, Ken Shoemake introduced their use to computer graphics.

Figure 22-6: Quaternion proponents
(used with permission)

189

In computer graphics, the quaternion is usually expressed as [v, w], where $v = (x, y, z)$ corresponds with the (I, J, K) scalars; w is the Re scalar. The *conjugate* of q is $q* = [-v, w]$.

Like a complex number, a quaternion is a rotation operator, but in three dimensions. v represents the axis of rotation and w the degree of rotation. Scalar multiples of a quaternion represent the same rotation, so it is convenient to work with unit-length quaternions (i.e., $|q| = x^2+y^2+z^2+w^2 = 1$).

Just as a complex number can be represented by an arc on the unit circle, a quaternion can be represented by a great arc on the unit sphere. The axis of rotation v passes through the origin, normal to the plane of the arc. The length of the arc corresponds to the degree of rotation (in actual fact, the arc length w spans half the angle of rotation).

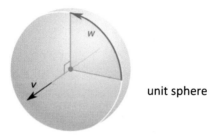

unit sphere

Figure 22-7: Quaternion rotation

Hamilton defined quaternion multiplication in a form similar to complex multiplication. For $q_1 = [v_1, w_1]$ and $q_2 = [v_2, w_2]$, the product $q_1q_2 = q = [v, w]$ is

$$v = w_1v_2 + w_2v_1 + v_1 \times v_2$$
$$w = w_1w_2 - v_1 \bullet v_2$$

Just as complex multiplication can be visualized as the combination of circular arcs, the product of quaternions can be visualized as the combination of spherical arcs (the arc can be freely slid along its great circle). As shown in the next figure, q_2q_1 represents the *composite rotation* produced by a rotation q_1 followed by a rotation q_2.

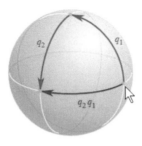

Figure 22-8: Quaternion multiplication

22.3 Quaternion as an Orientation

A quaternion can also be considered a rotation of the Cartesian coordinate system and, thus, an *orientation*. If q_1 and q_2 are different orientations, they can be represented as great arcs emanating from the same point.

Figure 22-9: Quaternion interpolation

Figure 22-9 is the same geometry as for multiplication (Figure 22-8), except the q_1 arc is reversed. Thus, the quaternion that transforms q_1 to q_2 is like multiplication, except the conjugate q_1^* is used. With multiplication, the result connects the tail of one arc to the head of another. But with orientation interpolation, the result connects two heads.

$q_2q_1^*$ is the unique rotation guaranteed to exist by Euler's *Rotation Theorem*. If q_1 and q_2 are reference frames, intermediate frames are produced by interpolation along the great arc $q_2q_1^*$. This *spherical linear interpolation* (called *slerp* by Shoemake) yields the dashed arcs in Figure 22-9, which are intermediate orientations between q_1 and q_2.

191

22.4 Comparison with Euler Angles

In Figure 22-1, the Euler angle traces are nonplanar; the rotation axis wobbles during the Euler angle interpolation. In comparison, the same rotation using quaternions produces traces that are planar, i.e., the rotation axis is constant.

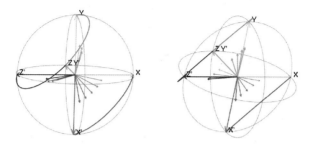

Figure 22-10: Quaternion interpolation, oblique view (left) and side view

Furthermore, the extraction of a quaternion from a matrix is not ill-defined, as it is for the extraction of Euler angles.

22.5 Quaternion Interpolation for Matrices

A matrix can represent a reference frame or a transformation; similarly, a quaternion can represent an orientation or a rotation. As with matrices, the multiplication of two quaternions can be interpreted as the rotation of an orientation (i.e., reference frame), or a composite rotation.

During key-frame animation, two reference frames f_1 and f_2 may be interpolated with the following code, which relies on Quaternion.h:

```
mat4 QuatInterpolate(mat4 f1, mat4 f2, float t) {
    Quaternion q1(f1), q2(f2), q; // convert matrices to quaternions
    q.Slerp(q1, q2, t);           // interpolate quaternions
    mat4 m = q.GetMatrix();       // set result's orientation
    vec4 p = (1-t)*f1[3]+t*f2[3]; // interpolate position
    for (int i = 0; i < 3; i++)   // set result's origin
        m[i][3] = p[i];
    return m;                     // return interpolated matrix
}
```

This is an interpolation between key reference frames. At the keys themselves, an abrupt change in the axis of rotation can occur. A higher-order interpolation can reduce this problem.

22.6 Camera Orientation

Quaternions can form the basis of a camera *arcball* that, unlike with Euler angles, cannot experience gimbal lock.

Further, it is simpler to store the camera *modelview* matrix as a single entity, rather than individual parameters (Euler angles, scale, and translation). The matrix can then be modified with quaternions that are created ab initio during user interaction.

Additional rotation about the z-axis may be needed to minimize camera tilt (which can be visually unsettling).

22.7 Exercise: A Quaternion Arcball

To incorporate quaternion rotation into our application, we define an Arcball class, and place an instance in the Camera class. The arcball will replace the rotation, but not the translation, functions of the original camera.

The Arcball class stores the following elements; the center, radius, and mouse locations are in pixels, and *m* is a pointer to the *modelview* matrix.

```
mat4 *m;                            // adjust upper left 3X3 of m
Quaternion qstart;                  // m's orientation on mouse down
vec2 center;                        // arcball screen center
float radius;                       // arcball screen radius
vec2 mouseDown, mouseMove;          // mouse down/drag
```

The application's mouse-down procedure can test whether the user picked the arcball:

```
vec2 dif(x-center.x, y-center.y);
bool selected = dot(dif, dif) < radius*radius;
```

The Arcball should contain mouse-down, mouse-up, and mouse-drag routines, to be called by the corresponding camera procedure. The *Down* subroutine initializes both *mouseMove* and the quaternion that represents the orientation of the matrix *m*:

```
void Arcball::Down(int x, int y) {
    mouseDown = mouseMove = vec2(x, y); // mousedown, disable arc
    if (m)
        qstart = Quaternion(*m);
}

void Arcball::Up() {
    mouseDown = mouseMove = vec2(0, 0); // disable arc display
}
```

The *Drag* subroutine uses the mouse-down and mouse-drag locations to compute two vectors; each vector originates at the center of the arcball and terminates at a 3D point on a virtual sphere computed from the mouse location.

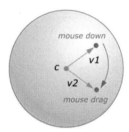

Figure 22-11: Mouse down and mouse drag on the virtual arcball sphere

The following routine calculates the vector given a point within the arcball circle:

```
vec3 Arcball::BallV(vec2 mouse) {
    // return vector from arcball center to point on arcball sphere
    vec2 dif(mouse-center);
    float difLen = length(dif);
    if (difLen > .97f*radius)          // if mouse exceeds radius
        dif *= (.97f*radius/difLen);  // constrain to circumference
    float sq = radius*radius-dot(dif, dif);
    vec3 v(dif.x, dif.y, sqrt(sq));   // in pixels
    return normalize(v);
}
```

The cross product of the two vectors yields an axis of rotation and the dot product determines the degree of rotation; these form a quaternion representing the user's intended rotation. It is applied to matrix *m* by multiplying the rotation quaternion with the quaternion representing the initial reference frame implied by *m* (i.e., on mouse down). The upper 3 by 3 elements of *m* are rewritten, representing the new orientation of *m*. This removes any scaling that may have been in *m*, but does not affect translation.

```
void Arcball::Drag(int x, int y) {
    mouseMove = vec2(x, y);
    vec3 v1 = BallV(mouseDown), v2 = BallV(mouseMove);
    vec3 axis = cross(v2, v1);
```

```
    if (dot(axis, axis) > .000001f) {
        float angle = (float) acos((double) dot(v1, v2));
        Quaternion qrot(axis, angle);
        Quaternion q = qstart*qrot;
        mat3 m3 = q.Get3x3();
        // rewrite rotation terms (upper 3 by 3) of m
        for (int i = 0; i < 3; i++)
            for (int j = 0; j < 3; j++)
                (*m)[i][j] = scale*m3[i][j]; // scale prev computed
    }
}
```

Finally, a draw subroutine allows the application to display the arcball:

```
void Arcball::Draw(mat4 fullview) {
    if (m == NULL)
        return;
    UseDrawShader(ScreenMode()); // all in pixels
    vec3 v1 = BallV(mouseDown), v2 = BallV(mouseMove), s1;
    // draw arc
    if (length(mouseDown-mouseMove) > 2)
        for (int i = 0; i < 24; i++) {
            vec3 m = v1+((float)i/23)*(v2-v1);
            vec3 v = radius*normalize(m);
            vec3 s2(center.x+v.x, center.y+v.y, 0);
            if (i > 0)
                Line(s1, s2, 2, vec3(1,0,0));
            s1 = s2;
        }
    // draw outer circle
    vec3 p1(center.x+radius, center.y, 0), p2;
    for (int i = 1; i < 36; i++) {
        float a = 2*3.141592f*((float)i/35);
        p2 = vec3(center.x+radius*cos(a),center.y+radius*sin(a),0);
        Line(p1, p2, 2, vec3(1,0,0));
        p1 = p2;
    }
}
```

22.8 Exercise: An Arcball for Multiple Meshes

Allow interactive positioning/orienting of multiple models: use Mover for position and Arcball for orientation.

Index

197

200

Volkswagen 78

Warnock, John 77, 147
Watkins, Gary 85
WebGL 6-8
weighting 139, 140
Williams, Lance 103, 117, 118
wrinkled 120

x-axis 44, 47, 48, 50, 51, 60, 142, 150, 152

Xerox PARC 2, 147
xy-plane 46, 120, 122, 162, 171

yaw 51, 185
y-axis 44, 47, 48, 50, 51, 60, 142, 152, 187

z-axis 43, 44, 49, 51, 60, 61, 63, 67, 71, 97, 142, 152, 187, 193
z-buffer 3, 66, 67, 166

verismilitode
photorealism

Made in the USA
Middletown, DE
14 September 2019